A
Shadow in My
Life

Rita Jerram

Stairwell Books and Fighting Cock Press

Published by Stairwell Books and Fighting Cock Press
70 Barbara Drive
Norwalk
CT 06851 USA

161 Lowther Street
York, YO31 7LZ

and

Fighting Cock Press
45 Middlethorpe Drive
York, YO24 1NA

Original Fighting Cock logo by Stanley Chapman

ISBN: 978-1-939269-54-6

Printed and bound in UK by Russell Press
Layout design: Alan Gillott
Edited by Pauline Kirk

Dedicated to all those tubercular patients who didn't get to live their lives.

Rita Jerram

Table of Contents

Foreword   1
A New Patient   3
Paint and Powder   8
Second Best (Dottie's Story)   10
The Christmas Box   15
Home Sweet Home (Angie's Story)   17
The Treatments   23
A Special Treat   26
A Precious Gift (Babs' Story)   30
A Taste of Freedom   34
A Little Holiday (Nan's Story)   39
An Afternoon Matinee   42
The Spoils of War (Elsa's Story)   48
Duty Calls (Sister McIvor's Story)   54
New Year's Eve   59
Knitting for Angels (Janet's Story)   62
A Cuckoo in the Nest   65
Goodbye Momma (Rebecca's Story)   69
Visitors   73
A Hard Life (Amy's Story)   77
The Redhead   84
A Special Mark (Eva's Story)   87
A Little Bit of Pampering   90
A Gentle Giant (Miss Hopper's Story)   93
A Shared Romance   97
Sister McIvor's Holiday   100
A Bright Star Shining (Gwen's Story)   104
Coronation Day 1953   108
An Unexpected Visitor   110
Waiting for the Postman (Ruth's Story)   113
The Easter Bride (Eileen's Story)   116
Food for Thought (My Story)   120
The Good Samaritans   123
The Facts of Life   126
Going Home   129
Cured   132
Memories   134
Editors' Note   137

Foreword

A Shadow in My Life is part memoir, part biography, based in the early fifties, when I was a patient in a tubercular Sanatorium in Staffordshire. It tells the stories of twelve women, thrown together in shared adversity as patients on the balcony of a women's ward.

It shows the desperate unity we shared, and how we became so close in the months of bed rest and treatment that a tight family unit was formed. It portrays both the sadness, and the ever-present humour that our enforced relationship produced.

Sanatoriums are now a relic of the past. They were established in the 1940s for patients suffering from Tuberculosis. Patient survival rates were very low. The "treatment" at this time involved long periods in bed, with fresh air as the only cure. Wards were therefore open on one side, or on a veranda. The drug Streptomycin was formulated towards the end of the Second World War and became, in time, a successful cure. In the forties and fifties, however, a stay as a patient in a Sanatorium could last for long periods, often years, and rarely less than eighteen months. This lengthy hospitalisation created a tight family atmosphere amongst patients of various ages and backgrounds. It united patients in a fight for recovery. Fortunately, the disease can now usually be cured, with four to nine months of antibiotics.

My generation is the last of that time when people were incarcerated for long stretches of bed rest, and my memories give a valuable insight into an era now forgotten. The eighteen months when I was an inmate of the Sanatorium was a wonderful finishing school, giving me life again, but also a strong insight and gratitude for my recovery. It created a bond between the people who were able to live their lives, and sad remorse for the ones who couldn't.

We told each other our life stories, and explained how we came to be patients in the Sanatorium. Lying in bed with only the flickering flames of the coke stove illuminating our faces, we shared secrets that otherwise would never be told. The staff too are very much part of the story. Sister McIvor was the epitome of the old-fashioned nursing sister, dedicated to her patients and their recovery.

1

This book is a tribute to those women who briefly shared my life, many of whom didn't get to live their own.

Rita Jerram.

A New Patient

In June 1953, I became a patient on Ward B. An earlier bout of pleurisy had left a shadow on my lung. My health was continuing to cause anxiety, so our family doctor decided to send me for a chest x-ray. The appointment came just two weeks after I had celebrated my 15th birthday. I was due to attend a chest clinic to have the x-ray, and afterwards to see a consultant to discuss the results. Little did I know with that admittance my life would change for ever.

It was a lovely sunny day when my mother and I arrived promptly for the 11 o'clock appointment, and I with the optimism of youth had no qualms about its outcome. With great difficulty we found the drab prefabricated building, which was tucked away in the old infirmary grounds. It was such an undistinguished structure that with first glance it simply couldn't be associated with what I realised later were the momentous life and death decisions that were made under its roof.

Here I met Dr Paul for the first time. He was the leading specialist in the area for Pulmonary Tuberculosis; a kindly looking middle aged man, who on our first acquaintance didn't fill me with the awe and trepidation that our further relationship would produce.

He believed in plain speaking, and without any hesitation told me that I had a tubercular shadow on my lung, which hopefully would respond to bed rest and a course of the newly discovered drug Streptomycin. I still didn't fully understand the repercussions of his brusque statement, and was horrified to hear him arranging over the phone for my immediate admittance to a Sanatorium.

I started to cry, feeling as if all control was being taken away from me. I knew I was ill, and throughout the past year whilst I had been suffering from the dire effects of Anorexia, part of me had been aware of the damage it was causing my health. But I alone had been in control of my destiny, which is the foremost element of that devastating illness.

Within the hour, and with no opportunity to say goodbye to my father and sisters I found myself in an ambulance being transported to the Sanatorium. My mother was following in a taxi, after hurriedly returning home to pack my nightwear. She and close family had all

3

been instructed to attend the clinic the next day for x-rays; exciting for my younger siblings but very shameful in my parents' eyes. They seemed to think there was a stigma attached to having a daughter with Tuberculosis.

As the ambulance drove through the busy shopping street I stared from the window at people going about their business, and envied them their health. When I saw the large iron gates of the Sanatorium closing behind us I felt a chill of fear, feeling as if I was going to be locked away for ever.

We drove up a long, winding hilly drive before coming to a stop outside Ward B. With trembling legs, I was helped down from the ambulance and taken into the ward's vast entrance hall. I had a view of long marble corridors which seemed to disappear towards unknown territory. A stiffly dressed figure approached from behind me, and in a soft Scottish accent said that she was Sister McIvor, and had been expecting my arrival. She led the way down one of the long corridors until we reached some double doors that led onto a wide veranda. The rustling of her starched white apron, the firm set of her frilly bonnet, and the firmness of her tread had quite unnerved me, and I was totally unprepared for the sight of the eleven occupied beds that spanned the length of the ward.

Sister McIvor led me to the empty twelfth one in the far corner, pulled some screens around it, and, not unkindly, told me to undress and get into bed. Too scared and shy to explain that I had no pyjamas until my mother arrived I simply did as I was told, undressed and climbed between the stiff sheets just wearing my knickers and vest. A nurse soon appeared behind the screen to take my pulse and temperature. She introduced herself as Nurse Bumstead and asked if I was feeling nervous. I was so close to tears I could only nod my head.

"You will soon settle down," she said. But I didn't want to settle down. I wanted to go home.

When my mother was eventually ushered to my bedside that was the first demand I tearfully made of her. "Please, please take me home," I begged.

She said it wasn't possible as I was infectious and she couldn't risk having me at home because of my sisters. I felt like a leper and cried even more. After she had left and I was decently clad, Nurse Bumstead removed the screens, leaving me exposed to the curious eyes of the other lepers. The ward was deadly quiet. Some were asleep, others were slumped down their beds, seemingly uninterested in the new arrival, and yet I felt I was under constant scrutiny. Finally I buried my head under the blankets, crying quietly until the bed felt quite damp.

At 2 p.m., Sister McIvor bustled onto the veranda and sharply rang a big brass bell. On its peals, the whole ward seemed to come alive. Patients sat up, alert and eager to talk. Questions were fired at me from the length of the room:

"What's your name?"

"Where are you from?"

"Have you been to the pictures recently?"

"Have you got a boyfriend?" The latter was from Gwen, who as I came to realise had an obsession about having a boyfriend.

I was utterly bewildered. Within seconds the veranda had become a vision of bedlam. The staff had failed to inform me that each day there was a morning and afternoon rest hour, and unfortunately I had been admitted during the latter one.

At first the babble of voices and the rapid firing of questions unnerved me, and I almost preferred the compulsory silence of the rest hour. Looking down the row of beds I realised that at fifteen I was probably the youngest there; I had escaped the children's ward only by my recent birthday. Those first few hours on the veranda I felt dreadfully alone as everyone seemed to have a close companionship, a feeling that reminded me of my first day at secondary school when as a late arrival I had found myself friendless and very much an outsider. During the past year, I had also, because of my Anorexia, allowed myself to relish isolation, and this sudden immersion into society was an ordeal, and one that I couldn't escape.

The only solitude I had that first afternoon were the brief visits to the bathroom which I cherished and extended for as long as I dare. Although once Sister McIvor had read my notes and seen the x-ray that had arrived from the clinic, I was denied this comfort as I had been put on complete bed rest.

That first evening I was surprised to see others who were also on strict bed rest hopping out of bed as soon as Sister McIvor disappeared down the drive at the end of her shift, and soon they had all gathered around my bed to continue their earlier inquisition. When I told them that I was only here for a few weeks they all laughed. "Dr Paul tells everyone that," they said, and went on to give me details of their own extended stay on Ward B. Some had been there for two years or more. Gwen held the record, having spent time on the children's ward before coming onto the veranda five years earlier. I was horrified by their stories and wrote a hasty letter to my father pleading with him to come and rescue me – immediately!

Those first two weeks were hard. The days seemed so long and tedious, the routine so restricting, and my shyness a serious handicap.

But with my fellow patients' kindness and compassion I slowly started to accept my incarceration, and became resigned to a lengthy stay.

The Sanatorium was built high on a hill overlooking rolling countryside. From a distance, it looked like a collection of large wooden cricket pavilions, with wide porches. All the buildings were open to the elements. Ward B, the women's section, had two large rooms and one smaller veranda. Twelve beds were pushed to the outer edge of this space, almost in touching distance of the towering pine trees that surrounded the building.

I was the youngest of the twelve women on the ward, whose ages ranged from fifty to my fifteen. I had a wonderful education from those diverse, inspiring women; not academic, but a tutoring of life that was priceless.

When evening came and the ward was lit only by the smouldering fire, conversations became more personal. They discussed their boyfriends, marriages, sex lives, and often secrets considered too shameful to be aired in the light of day.

I grew to love all of these women – we were closer to each other than we would ever be with our families. We quarreled, we argued, but we were all united in our fight against the shadow of death that was always lurking close by. Day by day we shared each other's lives. Ruth in the corner bed was madly in love with a postman from Walsall, and she believed each visiting day that he would come, but he never did. Eileen in the next bed had received a 'Dear John letter' from her fiancée which broke her heart. And Gwen, a beauty with long lustrous hair and flushed tubercular cheeks, lamented that at twenty she had never had a boyfriend – poor Gwen, she died a year later forever a virgin.

Next to me was Eva, a sad girl who had not been allowed to cuddle the baby she had recently given birth to, her infected lungs having been detected in early pregnancy. She cried herself to sleep every night with her baby's photograph in her hand. On my other side was Nan, a tired, worn out mother of six, who was secretly grateful for the enforced rest from her virile husband and demanding children. Angie, further up the veranda, was a generous loving woman who had been, in her own words, "an occasional lady of the night!" and she kept the ward enthralled with tales of her more un-orthodox clients.

Humour and laughter were often our only defense against the grim ravages of our shared disease. We lost Amy one night, her coughs and fevers proving too much for her weakened heart, and she slipped away in the early light. Her locker was cleared, the empty bed remade – yet another devastating reminder of our vulnerability.

A few weeks later we cheered and waved as Janet was driven off to Warwick hospital to have the infected part of her lung removed, her hoped-for new life about to begin. Later that day a nurse whispered that she had died during the operation. We were all inconsolable, and held each other tight, mourning Janet and fearful for our own futures.

With the aid of a new wonder drug called Streptomycin I was eventually cured, but it came too late for many of my loved fellow patients. After many months of complete bed rest and daily injections of the magical drug I was restored to health, and allowed to leave the Sanatorium. I have much to thank the disease for – it gave me an early insight into life and death, and made me realise just how precious life is.

Paint and Powder

We called the destructive bacteria that had invaded our bodies 'The Bug'. It had effectively curtailed our lives and thrown us together, without choice to languish on the open veranda of Ward B. But despite the greedy, vicious nature of the illness it never succeeded in destroying our spirit. Life in the Sanatorium was not all tears and sadness; there was much warmth and shared laughter in our enforced sisterhood.

Visiting day, which consisted of one and a half hours each Sunday afternoon, was anticipated with the excitement that only participants of complete bed rest could generate. Preparations would begin days before, with the more robust patients washing and ironing the finery which we all had in our lockers and saved for special occasions. Blouses, earrings and make up were swapped and shared, and Saturdays were completely given over to face packs and manicures. And finally in the evening we would dampen and pin-curl our hair, quite prepared for an uncomfortable night's sleep, but accepting the discomfort in return for a glorious head of curls the next morning.

We were an impressive sight when the visitors arrived, all powdered and perfumed, our top halves smart with no glimpse of the ugly flannelette pyjama bottoms which were well hidden under the bedclothes. With all this glamour and our flushed tubercular cheeks we looked far healthier than the poor visitors, who had struggled the mile up the hill from the nearest bus stop to arrive panting and wheezing at our bedsides, most having worn extra layers of clothing to combat the often arctic breezes that blew across our terrace.

Some patients had rare visits, having come to the Sanatorium from further afield, and often unsuspecting visitors were shared out and distributed around the ward. The exchange of local gossip passing from bed to bed gave the impression to visiting newcomers of our being one large extended family.

When the last visitor had left we pooled our gifts. The homemade cakes, fruit and sweets were divided equally amongst us all, and books, jigsaws and magazines placed on the communal table for all to share. With the excitement over, Sunday evenings always seemed flat, with everyone feeling out of sorts. It was as if our tight knit group had been invaded by outside influences, enjoyable at the time, but leaving a taste of resentment when they returned to that world which was denied to us. They had disturbed our solidarity, bringing unwanted irritation to our narrow lives. The veranda would be unusually quiet as we reflected on our endless captivity. But eventually someone would crack a joke or repeat some amusing gossip, and this would dispel the gloom, and soon we would be talking about what to wear next Sunday.

The most important dates on the ward's calendar were the monthly visits of Dr Paul, the Sanatorium's consultant. Out came our finery again, and any pallor was disguised with rouge, and fiery cheeks toned down with powder. The bed covers were changed, and staff sporting freshly starched caps and aprons would line up for Sister McIvor's inspection. Our locker tops would be cleared of clutter, and the newly polished floor given a final buff.

This was no ordinary doctor's round. This was a visitation from "God", our futures depending on his words of wisdom. All eyes followed him as he made his majestic way down the veranda, surrounded by his devoted followers. He stopped at each bed in turn, studying x-rays and passing divine judgements. If the news was good we would all smile and softly applaud, but would be instantly silenced by a quelling glance from Sister McIvor.

When he reached my bed I hardly dared breathe or raise my eyes to his imposing presence. Time seemed to stand still whilst he studied my latest x-ray and daily charts, and then I heard the magic words, "To be allowed up Sister, for bathroom visits."

Oh joy! I was to be released from total bed rest at last. As he moved on I whispered, "Thank you God."

Second Best (Dottie's Story)

At fifty, Dottie was the eldest patient on the ward. She was tall and gaunt, her face heavily lined. She looked intimidating, but was in fact very kind and always the one we turned to when distressed or needed advice. She wasn't a motherly soul and gave no comforting hugs, but you always knew that she would tell you the absolute truth, and that her common sense and clear thinking would help solve your problems or enable you to deal with them. Dottie's wisdom came from a lifetime's observation of the social behaviour of the public with whom she had always worked.

Originally from a rural background, she had spent most of her working life in the service industry, starting as a chambermaid at the Queen's Hotel when she first left school. Country girl she might have been, but she was never naive or lacking in intelligence, and with the strict morality that her god-fearing mother had installed in her, was well able to deter and repel the over-familiar commercial travellers who were the hotel's main clientele. Dottie was nobody's fool, and, heeding her mother's stern cautions, had no intention of getting herself in trouble.

She took pride in her work and was well thought of by the hotel's housekeeper. She had a slim, neat figure and smooth long brown hair which she always wore swept up and twisted into a net. She made a point of dressing well, opting for one good outfit rather than having many of lesser quality. Her shoes were always well polished and were taken regularly to the cobbler to be soled and heeled. Meticulous about her own appearance and hygiene, she couldn't bear the messy state that some of the less fastidious hotel guests left their rooms in.

Her one recreation was dancing, and she would visit afternoon tea dances with Elsie, her friend and fellow chambermaid. Being a good dancer she was never short of partners, but didn't encourage any intimacy or look for possible liaisons amongst them. She would gracefully waltz or quickstep around the floor, her body attuned to the music, but always with one eye on the clock, not wanting to be late for her evening duties. Her devotion to work had been noted by the hotel management who gave her the opportunity to acquire other skills, and soon she could turn her hand to most tasks in the hotel: serving behind the bar when needed; acting as relief waitress if required; and even cooking fifty breakfasts in an emergency. She was happy enough with her life; the small dramas and everyday occurrences of a busy hotel didn't allow for boredom.

By her twentieth birthday she had gained the position of assistant housekeeper and was well respected by her fellow staff and regular guests. It was about this time that Philip Atkins came into her life. He had booked into the Queen's for a week; he was taking up a new position at a local bank, and needed time to find lodgings in the area. Dottie admired his smart appearance, his softly spoken southern accent and the courtesy and consideration he showed at all times to the hotel staff. His room was always left tidy, personal belongings out of sight, and his spotless hairbrushes and shaving kit placed neatly on the dressing table, no screwed-up damp towels lying on the floor, and his wash basin always cleared of facial hair. Dottie had a horror of gentlemen guests and their unmentionable habits with wash basins. She felt Mr Atkins was a man with her own finesse and impeccable good taste.

He seemed to go out of his way to talk to her, and she found herself lingering outside his room hoping to catch sight of him as he left for work. She missed him when he found lodgings and moved out, but was thrilled when he started to come into the hotel bar after the bank had closed, always searching her out. She grew used to him popping his head round the housekeeper's door, and his shy smile when seeing her. Dottie realised that he liked her, and was not surprised when he asked her to accompany him to the theatre on her next night off. They had a pleasant evening; he was an attentive escort, holding her arm to cross the street, buying her chocolates before taking their seats, and having the forethought to have ordered coffee and biscuits for the interval.

She thought him the most agreeable and nicest man she had ever met, and after further theatre visits and an occasional Sunday afternoon stroll in the park, she came to the conclusion that he was courting her. He didn't make her heart flutter or bring goose pimples to her skin as Elsie's 'True Love' magazines said he should, but he was well groomed, respectful, and in a good steady job with excellent prospects. She felt she could do worse, and returned his next tentative peck on her cheek with a little more warmth and encouragement.

Six months later they married, and after an unexciting honeymoon in Southport, they started their married life in a small rented villa within walking distance of the bank. Dottie missed her busy life at the

Queen's, but enjoyed being mistress of her own home, and having Elsie round for tea to admire and envy her handsome wedding gifts, particularly the bone china tea service presented to her by the proprietors of the hotel. It was beautiful, a lustrous delicate china with a pink rosebud pattern. She would never use it, the set being far too precious for everyday use, but would always treasure it. She also enjoyed hearing Elsie's gossip about the hotel's staff and customers, but always felt a little dispirited after her friend had returned to work, almost resenting the lively chatter about a place that had been so important to her, and in which she no longer had a part.

Once the initial excitement of being married had passed, she began to find her new husband rather dull and boring. They no longer went to the theatre or for walks in the park. He had no interests or hobbies, and after their evening meal was finished he would settle in the armchair with the evening paper, reading it from cover to cover. Even the smallest of advertisements held his ardent attention. He would answer Dottie's eager attempts at conversation with grunts or a nod of his head, his face remaining hidden behind the paper. He repeatedly sucked his teeth and clicked his tongue, an irritating habit she had never noticed before their marriage, and which was now driving her mad after only a few months of his more intimate company.

He enjoyed her excellent cooking and domestic skills, always complimenting her on his perfectly ironed shirts and the spotless house. But that was the real problem. She didn't feel like a wife; she felt like his housekeeper. He seemed to take little notice of her as a person, seeming unaware of her needs. She felt quite relieved when he started to take an interest in politics and joined the local Liberal Club, attending meetings and lectures, always staying on for a drink afterwards with his new associates. Dottie was very lonely. A child might have made a difference, but that probability seemed unlikely. She couldn't bring herself to tell anybody, but he seemed to have lost interest in her in that way. On reflection, she realised that he'd never been passionately interested. Even the honeymoon had been lukewarm. She had put it down to their shared inexperience and his gentle modest manner.

By their first anniversary Dottie had accepted that she had made a mistake in marrying Philip. He was a good provider and had always treated her with the utmost respect, but she wanted more. She wanted to feel like a woman who was loved.

Things came to a head the following Easter when Dottie went to visit her family for the weekend. Philip had declined the joint invitation giving important business at the Liberal Club as his reason. Looking forward to a break from him she went alone. As usual twenty-four hours spent with Dottie's mother was enough and she decided to cut her visit short and return home. Arriving back late, having caught the last bus, she assumed that Philip would be out attending to his business at the club. She walked briskly home longing for a cup of tea, and a chance to put her feet up.

Opening the front door she was surprised to see a bicycle in the hallway and a coat she didn't recognise hanging on the peg. He must have a visitor she thought, who had gone with him to the meeting; strange, he had never had anyone visit him before. She shrugged, and went upstairs to unpack, pushing open the bedroom door with her bag whilst idly removing the pins from her hat. She was totally unprepared for the scene that confronted her – Philip lying naked and fast asleep on their bed, his arms and legs lovingly entwined around another naked figure. She gave a loud gasp and fled back down the stairs, shaking from head to toe, unable to believe what she had seen.

A few minutes later a fully clothed Philip came down the stairs closely followed by his intimate companion, who was still struggling to match buttons with their respective buttonholes. Dottie gasped again, and stared open mouthed when she recognised Eric Powell, the bank manager and prospective Liberal candidate for the next local election.

"I understood then why they called it the Liberal Club," she laughingly told us many years later on the veranda. "Easy to laugh now," she said, but at the time she had felt mortified and humiliated, although also very relieved when later that night Philip packed his belongings and without a word left her and the house for good.

Dottie went back to her old job at the Queen's, telling no one why her marriage had failed. She never saw Philip again, but heard a few weeks later that he had left the bank and moved back to the South, closely followed by his manager Mr Powell. She had remained in the little house, taking a gentleman lodger to help with her expenses. It seemed as if she had never married or been away from the hotel. She was very happy to be back and the proprietors equally pleased to have her. Eventually she was offered the head housekeeper's job, and stayed in that position for the next thirty years, content and highly regarded by all. And if she occasionally invited one of her discreet gentlemen lodgers to share her bed, no one ever knew or would have blamed her if they had.

Her Tuberculosis was discovered when the hotel staff were invited to attend a mobile x-ray unit, which was parked in the Queen's car park. Three weeks later she was occupying a corner bed on Ward B.

Dottie was a patient there for two years, and made a full recovery. On her release from the Sanatorium she moved into a small council flat, and after a period of rest and convalescence went back to her beloved Queen's as a waitress, working there until the sad day when the hotel was sold and turned into luxury flats.

She was still working in her late seventies, helping out at wedding functions and private events. One evening she collapsed between courses, and died of a massive stroke whilst serving a private dinner at the Liberal Club. I'm sure if allowed a few moments grace before succumbing, she would have appreciated the irony of her final place of work.

The Christmas Box

As my first Christmas on Ward B approached I found myself caught up in the general excitement that the season created. Our beds were covered in the endless paper chains that we had all been urged to make as part of our daily occupational therapy. For many weeks we had spent hours poring over catalogues, choosing gifts for our families and each other. Eventually, after much deliberation, the order was sent off and its delivery anxiously awaited.

At last, one late December afternoon the delivery van arrived, and two young men struggled on to the veranda with a large box which they maneuvered into place under the Christmas tree. With backward bashful glances at the twelve eager females staring avidly at the results of their labours they made a hasty exit, with Gwen's strident wolf whistle ringing in their ears.

We were all anxious to open the box and inspect our chosen gifts, but at that moment the bell rang to announce supper time, and even patients fortunate enough to have some hours up had to return to bed. Our desire to see the box's contents was overshadowed by our fear of Sister McIvor. Her strict routine always had to be adhered to – she was ex-army, and when disobeyed had a voice that could crack ice at fifty yards, and a piercing glance that made you shiver and shrink into your pyjamas. No one had the courage to defy her orders.

Somehow we endured supper, sustained with the hope that Sister McIvor would relent and allow us to open the box before she went off duty. But we were disappointed. She insisted that we stay in bed, and before handing over to the night staff gave us a pep talk about not allowing our bugs to get excited.

Until Night Sister switched off the lights at 9 p.m., our eyes never strayed from the enticing shape of that tantalizing box. Having been pre-warned by Sister McIvor, she stood with her hand on the switch and warned us to get straight off to sleep, and give our agitated bugs a rest.

We settled down after some initial grumbling about over-officious staff, and all feeling very despondent at having the box so near, and as yet, unopened. But after a while the rebellious muttering died down,

15

and some were almost asleep, when, with a sudden flinging back of her bedclothes, quiet shy Eva jumped out of bed, shouting, "Bugger this! I'm getting my baby's presents out of that box." Within seconds everyone was out of bed, and tearing the box open, pulling the cartons out, tossing them in the air, dancing around the tree, all drunk with the excitement and release of our pent-up feelings.

Eva was holding her daughter's teddy bear tightly in her arms, crooning a lullaby to it, as if at last fulfilling the role that had been denied to her. Soon we were all running wildly up and down the veranda, some jumping from bed to bed. Someone put our one and only record onto the ward's ancient gramophone. It was Guy Mitchell singing 'She wore red feathers and a hula-hula skirt'. Gwen, snatching up the chiffon scarves that she had ordered for her sister's Christmas present, climbed onto the nearest bed and did the dance of the seven veils in time to the pounding music. We all clapped and urged her on.

When Sister McIvor appeared at the door, a stranger in her flannel dressing gown, and sandy hair in curlers, we must have presented a scene from her worst idea of hell. The flickering dying fire illuminated our pyjama clad figures frenziedly dancing, and our shrieks of hysterical laughter were rapidly turning into tubercular coughing. "Stop this madness at once," she cried, in a voice that would have put the toughest army recruit into abject terror.

We all froze, as if playing musical statues, all except of course Guy Mitchell, who was still singing about red feathers and hula-hula skirts, and Gwen, who in fright had dropped the last of her scarves and faced us all stark naked.

We stared at each other in shock, and then climbed sheepishly back into bed. Few noticed the twinkle in Sister McIvor's eyes or the twitch of her mouth as she hastily departed from the ward, leaving her twelve charges trying desperately to still their leaping hearts, and quench the fire of their startled bugs.

Home Sweet Home (Angie's Story)

Angie had a laugh that could be heard the length of the veranda. She also bleached her hair, which during the three months she had been on Ward B had started to show some dark roots. Her face was always powdered, and eyebrows plucked with a thin pencilled line taking their place, her lips a bright crimson slash that over-lapped her natural lip-line. She was blowsy, loud, and quite common, as Babs was often heard to remark. But I loved her. She was kind, warm and affectionate, always ready to listen to my woes, and comfort me when I felt depressed, having a great empathy that others lacked.

Some visitors muttered amongst themselves. "It's a disgrace," they said, "that the likes of her should be put on a ward with decent people." Angie was a local girl, and her reputation well known. The uncharitable gossips spoke of her being over-friendly with the American servicemen stationed nearby during and after the war, and it was whispered: "Even the black ones!"

Angie's mother had died when she was born, and a few years later she lost her father too, he falling victim to an influenza epidemic which swept the town one bitter winter. After his funeral she was taken to live with her grandmother. The next six years were the happiest of Angie's life; she loved her nan, and felt safe and secure when cuddled up to her in the large feather bed. But Nan was getting older, her legs were bad and she found it difficult looking after an active child. So Angie was passed around the family like an unwanted parcel, never feeling she really belonged anywhere. She became self-reliant at an early age, always aware that no home was permanent and that she was only there because of the generosity of her relatives.

The longest she stayed with anyone were the two years she lived in her aunt Dora's chaotic household. There she was just another mouth to be fed alongside the unruly mob of her own children that her aunt did her best to ignore. She left there hungry, her hair swarming with head lice and considerably dirtier than when she had first arrived. She was rescued from Aunt Dora by Uncle Jim, a paternal uncle she had never met. In his respectable lace-curtained villa she was never hungry,

17

and had a weekly bath in her Aunt Mary's spotless kitchen, into which no tenacious head louse would ever dare invade.

Angela, as the prim fastidious couple insisted on calling her, was very unhappy. Uncle Jim had been a sergeant major in the regular army, and ran his home as precisely as he had his barracks. There was a timetable for every second of the day. Her timid aunt's eyes never strayed far from the clock by which their lives were ruled. If Angie was a minute late from school or not prompt in taking her place at the dining table, Uncle Jim's belt would be unbuckled, and he would lash her legs with it, taking a chilling pleasure in doing so. Angie struck back at him once, hitting him about the chest with her shoe, screaming the obscenities acquired at Aunt Dora's knee. He stood unmoving, his face like thunder, staring at the wretched child that he had unwillingly taken into his home. He lifted her bodily and thrust her into the broom cupboard, locking the door from the outside. When a chastened Angie was released she saw her small suitcase packed and waiting by the door, her weeping aunt holding out her coat. "You are to go to your mother's brother," she whispered.

"Good," retorted Angie. "I hate it here, and I hate Uncle Jim, I wish he was dead." Unrepentant, she was escorted by a silent Uncle Jim on to the trolley bus, and deposited without a word at the front door of her new home.

She had vague memories of her mother's brother and his wife, having met them when they attended her father's funeral. She had no recollection of their names, and until she found herself on their doorstep, no idea of their location. Her new guardians were Uncle Samuel and Aunt Bridget, a God-fearing couple who, belated as it was, felt it their Christian duty to take in the orphaned child.

They introduced Angie to their only son who at fifteen was two years her senior. The spotty faced youth leered at his newly found cousin, who felt a little daunted at the prospect of sharing his home. Uncle Samuel was a cooper by trade, crafting stout oak barrels for the nearby brewery. He was also a lay preacher at the local Methodist church. His wife, the daughter of a clergyman, was as devoted as he, spending much of her time on church business. Eric, their precious son, whom God had given them late in life, was at grammar school and they had great ambitions for him.

The house was clean, but cold, the food plentiful but dull, as were her new relatives, so Angie thought. She was unwillingly taken to church three times a day each Sunday, often suffering the powerful booming voice of her uncle damning the immoral and condemning the un-believers. Feeling bored, she tried to catch the eye of a good

18

looking boy in the next pew, but was firmly reprimanded by her aunt, who, despite her devout expression, missed nothing. Even worse was to come. She was enrolled into a young girls' Christian group which met every Thursday evening. None of this was to Angie's liking, but she was never consulted. When invited to the cinema by a new school friend, she decided to exchange a pious two hours at the church hall for the delights of the Odeon. It was unfortunate that as they came out blinking in the sudden daylight, cousin Eric was passing by, returning home from his extra maths tuition. He cycled alongside the girls. Angie begged him not to tell his parents, and with a gloating smirk on his face he agreed. But before turning into their yard he warned her that she would owe him a big favour if he was to say nothing about her escapade.

This obligation was called for the very next night. With his father nodding over his bible at the kitchen table, and his mother out on one of her errands of mercy, Eric crept upstairs, carefully avoiding the middle squeaky step, and stopping at the top listening for the sound of his father's snoring. Reaching his cousin's door he gently pushed it slightly ajar, and pressing his face to the gap, drooled at the sight of Angie in her underwear preparing for bed. Unaware of the 'peeping Tom', she completely disrobed giving her cousin's adolescent hormones a sudden surge which propelled him into her room, where he clutched her to his puny body. Angie pushed him away, giving him a stinging slap across his face, and, bringing up her knee, forcibly kicked him in an appropriate place. Eric stumbled out of the room, his ardour somewhat cooled, and collided with his father who was rushing up the stairs in answer to his son's agonised cries. Eric quickly gave his account of the events, suggesting that his cousin had invited him into her room. "She's been making eyes at me for weeks," he said.

A hasty family conference was called when Aunt Bridget returned, from which Angie was excluded. It was decided that she would have to go. Christian charity was cast aside without regret – she was a bad influence, corrupting and enticing their beloved son. Angie, securing her door, had already had her own solitary conference and had reached a similar conclusion. She couldn't stay with this hypocritical smug family any longer. She was almost fourteen, which was the legal age she could leave school, but she could easily pass for sixteen. She decided she would find a job and a room to rent, and look after herself in future.

Early the next morning, tightly gripping her small suitcase, she left the tall gloomy house for ever, and standing by the gate looked back and shouted, "I hope you all go to hell, hallelujah." At the bus terminal she climbed aboard the first bus she saw, enjoying the taste of freedom, feeling carefree and happy. Arriving at the next town which was as far as her purse could stretch, she eagerly started her search for work. By mid-afternoon her spirit was flagging. No one seemed to want the homeless forlorn young girl clutching her shabby suitcase. Feeling exhausted by lack of food and her futile search, she decided to spend her last few coppers and have a cup of tea at the Riverside tea rooms. This decision changed her luck and her life. The manager was at that moment placing a card in the window asking for live-in staff. .Angie's cheerful smile and clean appearance, plus a little bit of twinkle in her eyes, persuaded him to give her a job on one month's trial.

Angie stayed there for eight years, rising to be head waitress, and with her cosy room in the attic of the cafe was very content and happy. Her ready smile and friendly manner had made her a popular waitress, and she had managed to save a good little nest egg with the generous tips she received – this gave her a feeling of independence and security. As she matured she had boyfriends, but never a serious relationship until, one busy lunch time she served a handsome dark haired stranger. Although slightly older than her usual admirers, she felt an immediate attraction, which he seemed to return. He lunched there daily, always sitting at Angie's table, and at the end of the week asked her out. He said he was a sales rep for the brewery and travelled all over the country. Angie fell deeply in love with him – all the years of her loneliness, and the tough front she had presented to the world dissolved. She gave her all to the lover which he had quickly become.

"To cut a long story short," she said, when telling us her life story one night on the veranda, her face illuminated by the fire light, "the bastard took everything – my love, my virginity, and every penny of my bloody savings."

It seemed he was married with four children, and a girlfriend in every town. After this experience Angie hardened her heart, and trusted no man. She left the tea rooms and returned to her home town, taking a job as a barmaid at the Station Hotel. She rented a small flat nearby – it was the first home that was really hers. Short of money, but not admirers, Angie decided she might as well be paid for what she had freely given to her lover. She was discreet and had a few regular clients, and was well able to afford the little luxuries she craved.

With the advent of the 'Yanks' as she called them, her life became more exciting. The war changed it completely. Working by day in the munitions factory and jitter bugging the nights away with the smart uniformed men who treated her like a lady, Angie was in her element.

She met Eddie one foggy night, bumping into him as she hurried home to change from her dirty overalls into a glamorous frock ready for another night of fun. He was a tall rangy Texan newly arrived in England. He was not good looking, but had a kind rugged sort of face with the bluest eyes Angie had ever seen. In the fog she didn't see any of these things, but felt comforted by the way he took her arm to guide her home, and the polite way he called her 'Ma'am'. He asked her out, and she found him a refreshing change from her other Yankee dates. With his Texan drawl he talked in a quiet measured way about his home and family back on their small ranch a few miles outside Lubbock. Angie could see by the faraway look in his eyes and the way he spoke that he was very homesick.

They became close. Eddie saw beneath her 'devil may care' attitude, and saw the real Angie; hurt, lonely, and afraid of growing old alone. He reached out to her, and she responded, becoming the warm, gentle girl she really was. The night before he left to go overseas they held each other close and talked about how when the war was over he would come back for her, and take her to Texas, and if she liked his little ranch and family he would ask her to stay and marry him.

She never heard from him again. At first she thought the letters were not getting through because of the battles, Eddie being in the forefront of the invasion forces. She remained faithful to him until V E Day, when she went out and got drunk, waking up the next morning with a nameless sailor by her side. She gradually put away any thoughts of Eddie, only to have them return after a few too many gin and oranges at the Rose and Crown, or alone in her flat when the memories of his blue eyes and gentle touch came back to haunt her, forcing her out to find some company or perhaps another lonely person.

About a year after the war ended she received a letter with an American stamp on the envelope. Opening it, a tattered creased photograph of her and Eddie fell out, their arms wrapped tightly around each other, both smiling happily at the camera. Through her tears Angie read the accompanying letter.

Dear Angela,

I found this snap of you and my son in the stuff that was returned to me after his death. He died a brave soldier according to his captain who wrote me after the war. I'm so proud of him, and from the letters that were in his kit, I guess you were too. I have enclosed his signet ring, which I know he would have wanted you to have. I will never get to meet you, but my heartfelt thanks for befriending my son in a strange land, and making his last days happy.

Yours in gratitude, Edith Gallio.

After this Angie gave up a little. She went to work each day, continued with her casual relationships, but became more careless in her appearance, neglecting herself and no longer caring what became of her life. By the time she became a patient on Ward B she was in a sorry state, her lungs riddled with Tuberculosis and her usual high spirits as low as they had ever been. The ambulance men brought her onto the veranda during the afternoon rest period when total silence prevailed. Once settled in her bed she gave a searching look around the ward – some of us sleeping, others quietly reading. "Oh God!" she said, "they've gone and put me in the morgue by mistake. Come on girls, give us a smile – you ain't dead yet."

Angie died six months later aged forty-two. She died peacefully with a smile on her face, fingering the signet ring on a silver chain around her neck.

I like to think that somewhere she and Eddie are together on their farm. God bless you, Angie, I love you, wherever you are.

The Treatments

If you were unfortunate enough to have Tuberculosis, at least the fifties was a better time to have it than any previous period in human history. Much progress had been made with both medication and in specialist knowledge. Streptomycin, a new so-called wonder drug, had recently been introduced, and was speeding up the recovery of many patients.

It was not suitable for every tubercular patient, and in some cases caused side effects which could be equally damaging. But it was the first time that medication had shown success in treating the illness. Previously the only known cure was a combination of bed rest with fresh air, and the many deaths that ensued were proof enough that it more often than not failed.

Other remedies were available and as a last resort the totally diseased lung could be removed surgically. This too had its dangers; a patient already weakened from the illness didn't always have the immunity or strength to counteract the effects of such a major operation, although many were successful and those patients did go on to live full and long lives with only one lung. Another procedure was to collapse a diseased lung and to have weekly infusions of gas or air. This action compressed the affected lung and forced it to rest to help promote healing. All of these practices were used during my time on the veranda.

I was one of the lucky ones who responded well to Streptomycin, which alongside the bed rest and fresh air cured the shadow on my lung. It was given daily by injection, and how those constant jabs were dreaded. The needles were big and clumsy and when forced into your buttock gave an immediate hard lump which often took hours to disperse, sometimes not fully disappeared when the next one was due. They caused a lot of discomfort, especially when on full bed rest. I had been known to hide in the bathroom when Sister McIvor appeared at the door with a covered tray in her hand, but she would demand that I return to bed immediately, and as much as I feared the injection I feared Sister more and would sheepishly unlock the bathroom door and climb back into bed, baring my bottom for yet another savage attack. On visiting day I would discreetly lift the bed clothes and display my bruised and swollen posterior, but received little sympathy from my mother. "It's for your own good" was the only response I ever got.

Regrettably Gwen was one of the unfortunate people whose lungs were so badly diseased that Streptomycin came too late to cure her. Despite her years in the Sanatorium and lack of recovery she never gave up, and her amazing spirit and zest for life was quite extraordinary. She always hoped that every new treatment would be the vital one for her. Dr Paul on his last visit had recommended she should have her lung collapsed. I think he was running out of remedies to save her, and would try anything possible to extend her life. As usual she used everything offered as a justification for leaving her bed, and if possible the veranda. She was delighted to have her lung collapsed. It meant a weekly trip up to the treatment room at the back of the men's ward. For Gwen this was an excuse to pile on make up, splash on the 'Evening in Paris' perfume which her sisters kept her well supplied with, and using her most effective weapon she would tighten her dressing gown belt to emphasise the breath-taking girth of her breasts. With both her lungs diseased, surgery was out of the question, and poor Gwen was doomed to rely on the old treatments of bed rest and fresh air, which after seven years had still not restored her to health. But be it a collapsed lung or x-rays she never missed an opportunity to flaunt her charms.

Ruth, Janet and Amy would accompany her each Monday morning to receive their air, and we lucky ones, as the rest of us on medication were thought to be, how we envied them their weekly trips to the treatment room! At least they got the chance to leave the confines of the ward.

Patients having their lung removed would be transported to Warwick Hospital. This was the nearest operating centre to our Sanatorium. We, left behind, couldn't imagine surviving a lifetime on one lung, but Sister McIvor said it was possible if the patient was sensible. Janet was unfortunate when she went to have her lung removed. Her stamina and determination were not enough to bring her through the operation.

Another sad loss that might have been prevented if the wonder drug had been found earlier! So many lost souls that could have been saved! But I give thanks for myself, and the many others for whom it came in time. Modern medicine has greatly reduced the disease from British waters. The Sanatoriums are long gone, leaving behind only the memories of people of a certain age who were confined in their breezy wards. The current treatments, which usually dispense with hospitalisation, consist of one or more drugs that have the patient healthy again in months. A recent rise in the disease is controlled, and hopefully we will never again see the devastating loss of life that previous numbers record[1].

[1] Unfortunately, this is no longer true. Please see Editors' Notes.

A Special Treat

"I have a special treat for you," said Sister McIvor coming out of her office and on to the veranda. "I've just had a phone call from the secretary of the Abbottsfield Colliery Male Voice Choir, and they have offered to come and sing for us." She went on to say that she had arranged for them to visit the following evening. "It's really good of them to take the trouble to come all this way. I hope you all appreciate that," she added. We must have looked dubious, because she gave us one of her looks and went back into the office.

We had been given these special treats before, and had become a little wary of them. Once it had been a group of Morris Dancers who had invaded the ward – rattling their sticks, and shaking ribbons and bells all over our beds for what seemed a never-ending demonstration of their talents. Despite our mass burrowing under the bedclothes they stayed on to give an encore, elated at having such a captive, immobile audience. When at last, with a final wave of their ribbons, they reluctantly left, we all had splitting headaches and raised temperatures, the latter most likely being from the amount of time we had spent hidden under our blankets.

Another special treat we were offered was given by two ladies who, as Sister McIvor pointed out, "have given up their precious time, both wanting to do something positive for the sick of the parish." Even she looked doubtful when they arrived. Both in their eighties and barely able to walk, it took an age for them to manoeuvre the steps up to the ward, and even longer to negotiate the expanse of polished floor before reaching our terrace. On arrival, they collapsed into the chairs that Sister McIvor had hurriedly provided. After a cup of tea and a rest, they said they felt well enough to begin. Gripping tightly to each other they stood up, and with many false starts recited some of their favourite poetry, doing all the appropriate gestures when required. Both nearly toppled over when the taller of the two, keen to emphasise with both arms a particularly dramatic line, briefly let go of her partner.

We clapped enthusiastically whenever they paused for breath, mistakenly thinking it was the end, but one of them would always start again, having remembered yet another verse. We were rescued from a lengthy ballad about 'Bonnie Prince Charlie' by Amy, who unfortunately suffered one of her violent coughing fits as it was about to begin. The dreadful sounds of her tortured lungs and the prolific use of her sputum cup was enough to bring the recital to a sudden end. The two ladies, suddenly realising the danger their good works had put them in, fled, making a remarkably speedy exit.

The best part of the afternoon's entertainment was yet to come, when Gwen and Babs did an impromptu but brilliant impersonation of the two fleeing ladies, mimicking their wavering voices and trembling knees to perfection. It was cruel, but very funny, and we all laughed until our sides hurt, the noise bringing Sister McIvor on to the ward, who reprimanded us for our lack of respect, and snidely reminded us of the damage such hilarity could do to our bugs.

Our biggest treat of all was the day 'The Great Dannillo' visited the ward, presented to us as a world-famous magician. He was, in fact, a white bearded elderly pensioner dressed in a rather seedy well-worn tuxedo. His equally aged wife was introduced as his exotic charming assistant. She wore a pink satin leotard, and on her skinny legs black fishnet tights, which when she did a twirl showed many gaping holes, plus a glimpse of her grey flannel bloomers. We realised halfway through the act that he was very drunk. His attempts to make his wife disappear had hilarious results. Every time he tapped the magic box it opened to show her still there, with a fixed smile, and her false teeth vibrating as she swayed in time to the non-existent music. We realised then that she was quite drunk too.

The climax of the show came when their sleepy white rabbit suddenly woke, and not waiting to be pulled out of 'The Great Dannillo's top hat, scampered off across the terrace. It caused chaos. The magician vented his drunken anger by cursing his wife, the rabbit, and us. When Sister McIvor came to see what the uproar was, he cursed her too. Whilst he stood, madly swearing and pulling endless coloured scarves from his secret pockets, his poor wife was crawling from bed to bed on all fours, gaining a few more holes in her tights as she went, softly calling "bunny, bunny, come to Mama."

The absconding rabbit was eventually found in Sister McIvor's office, chewing on the fluffy slippers that she secretly wore when writing reports at her desk. Thankfully after this incident we were given no further treats; that is until the Abbottsfield Colliery Male Voice Choir decided to visit us.

In anticipation of the choir having some personable young men we donned our finery and waited expectantly for their arrival. Promptly at 7 p.m., Sister McIvor ushered them into the ward, wearing a new frilly cap, we noted, and her high heels. After a steely glance in our direction she retired to her office, with Eileen's evening paper hidden under her apron. The choir, smartly dressed in their matching blue blazers and grey flannel trousers, assembled into their usual format. They seemed ill at ease, avoiding any direct eye contact with the twelve expectant females who were searching avidly for a sign of any good-looking young miners amongst them. After much foot shuffling and throat clearing they lifted their heads to sing. Catching our eyes for the first time, they seemed to be struck dumb, and stared at us as if viewing some strange new species at the zoo. We all stared fixedly back at them, watching the red flushes that were slowly staining their necks.

The choir was surprisingly good, and we enjoyed their selection of songs, but they made it obvious that we were not their choice of audience. Surely it wasn't necessary to use throat spray after every song, or to hold handkerchiefs to their mouths in between, or even become slightly apoplectic, as one of them did, trying to sing through his tightly fastened lips. We realised that these big tough miners were scared of us, terrified of catching our bugs.

It was Ruth who first started to giggle. She said afterwards that it was the little one on the front row, who looked like a monkey, and whose ears went up and down in time to the music. Every time she looked at him she couldn't help but laugh. She had a very infectious giggle that rapidly spread around the veranda. Within minutes we were all convulsed with silent laughter, stuffing towels or sheet corners into our mouths to stop it breaking free. It was mass hysteria, which was never far from the surface on Ward B.

The final straw was when Angie stage whispered, "That's him, the bald fat one at the back, he was my regular 6 o'clock every Friday night. You remember girls, I told you all about him, the one who always kept his hat on."

That did it. Our loud raucous laughter broke free – we roared, tears rolling down our cheeks, deep belly laughs that left you clutching yourself in pain. Eva said she had wet herself, and that made us worse. Sister McIvor stormed out of the office, reading glasses still perched on her nose, and a half-eaten chocolate digestive crumbling in her hand. She simply stared at us, speechless in shock and horror. The high notes of the choir's 'Jerusalem' slowly faded away as they too stared at us in dismay, Angie's friend on the back row trying hard to make himself invisible.

We became a little calmer when the music stopped, but there was still the odd titter that involuntarily escaped as the Abbottsfield Colliery Male Voice Choir left the ward, almost at a run, their faces showing the utmost relief Sister McIvor waved them off, her stiffened back expressing her anger more than words ever could.

We were all given a sleeping tablet that night, a sure sign of her great displeasure. The next morning she said she would never ever arrange another special treat for Ward B.

"Good," we all muttered.

A Precious Gift (Babs' Story)

Nellie and Harry Tomkins had waited many years for a child, and were both overjoyed when their daughter was born. Nellie, in her early forties, had given up any hope of ever getting pregnant, and after twenty years of marriage the couple had resigned themselves to being childless. The arrival of their little girl had seemed like a miracle – God's precious gift, Nellie's church-going mother always stated.

The happy pair doted on the pretty little girl – with her dimpled cheeks and blonde curly hair she was much admired by everyone who came into their village shop. They had run the general store for most of their married life, and were well known in the small mining village where it was situated.

They had thought long and hard about her name. Harry wanted to call her Alice after his mother, but Nellie had set her heart on calling her Barbara, being a keen cinema fan and a great admirer of Barbara Stanwyck. She got her way and the baby was duly christened, and for evermore became known as Babs.

The little family lived behind the shop, and Nellie would park the pram just inside the door of their living room, enabling her to serve customers and keep her eye on baby Babs at the same time. She was, fortunately, a good baby, and would lie for hours gurgling to herself, and flashing beaming smiles at any miner's wife who went to admire her. When she started to toddle, Harry fashioned a wooden gate which prevented her from wandering into the shop, and her besotted parents, between serving, would endlessly throw back the toys with which little Babs had delightedly littered the shop floor. Even at this tender age she recognised that a pitiful look of neglect would furnish her with an endless supply of sweets and biscuits, from parents and customers alike.

Nellie had high hopes for her daughter. She was determined that Babs would have every advantage that she could offer. She had put her name down for a private school, and envisaged dancing lessons, horse riding, and, looking to the future, a good secretarial college. She was adamant that no daughter of hers would end up serving behind a counter, or talk with the thick local accent that the village children shared. She urged Harry to expand the business; they made a good living from their little shop, but not good enough for such ambitious plans.

An old van was purchased and Harry converted it into a travelling shop, and whilst Nellie coped with the customers on her own, he spent his days driving around all the small outlying villages, offering groceries to a previously untapped clientele. Twice a week he finished early, returning to look after the shop whilst Nellie and Babs caught the bus into town to go to the pictures, both infatuated with the silver screen.

Babs loved going to the Misses Porter-Smith's private academy for young ladies. The weekly fees were far more than her parents could afford, but they were well satisfied with the results – their daughter was mixing with professional people's children. Her best friend's father was a doctor, and Nellie was overjoyed when Babs received an invitation to Margaret Fenton's birthday party. Her father was the local bank manager. This exclusive circle of friends and the lovely way that Babs spoke more than made up for the financial struggle that the Tomkins had. Harry had to travel further afield to find new customers, and Nellie extended the shop's opening hours, both determined to keep Babs happy.

Her father would drive her to town each morning and drop her off at the school gates, and proudly watch her walk up the drive in her smart uniform, swinging the real leather satchel that he had bought her as a birthday gift. As she got older she demanded to be dropped off around the corner, not wanting her friends to see the old green van with the words H&N TOMKINS GROCERIES, FRUIT & VEGETABLES painted on its side. She visited the homes of her school friends and envied their life-styles, lovely detached houses with lawns and flower beds, spacious bedrooms, and afternoon tea in the conservatory with dainty sandwiches, and home-made fairy cakes, their mothers smartly dressed, wearing make-up, and calling everybody 'darling'. She could never ask them back to her home – the tiny room at the back of the shop, her mother in a brown overall popping in and out of the kitchen whilst cooking dinner and serving customers at the same time, and then sitting down at the shabby oilcloth covered table to eat, only to have the shop doorbell ring again. She told her friends that mummy was an invalid and couldn't cope with visitors.

When Babs was thirteen her father had a terrible accident. Driving the van on an icy country lane, he skidded and hit a tree. Poor Harry lay unconscious surrounded by his dislodged fruit and vegetables until a passing farmer rescued him. The accident left him partially paralysed, no longer able to drive or do heavy lifting. Nellie worked even harder after this misfortune, desperately trying to keep Babs at her beloved school, but even she had to admit defeat when her sums told her it was impossible.

Babs hated the secondary school, she thought her new classmates vulgar, and did nothing to gain their respect. In fact they disliked her intensely. She corrected their English at every opportunity, insisted on calling dinner 'lunch', and showed her superior knowledge in every lesson.

Her greatest humiliation was having to help her mother in the shop. Wearing an old overall of her father's she unpacked provisions and stacked them on the shelves, and worst of all had to take out the orders on a rackety delivery bike, cycling through the village with her head down and desperately trying to ignore the snide remarks of her new classmates. Life as Babs knew it had come to an end.

Her only recreation was the twice weekly cinema trips that she now made alone, her mother tied to the shop, and her father sat in the back room with only the wireless for company. Her passion for films was her undoing. She had queued for hours in the rain to see a new Gregory Peck release and had got soaked to the skin before sitting in her wet clothes to see the film round again. A heavy cold quickly turned to pleurisy and Babs was very ill for many weeks. Her mother was exhausted, running the shop single handed and caring for her two invalids.

Babs seemed to take a long time recovering, and Nellie worried about the chesty cough and extreme tiredness that her daughter seemed unable to shake off. When a mobile x-ray unit visited the village she persuaded Babs to go and have a check-up. Two weeks later Babs joined us in Ward B.

She was just fifteen and Sister McIvor decided to put her in the next bed to me as I was the same age. But our years were the only thing we had in common – I was an avid reader of literature – she only read film magazines. I would spend days working on a jigsaw puzzle – she only wanted to gossip about film stars. We were totally incompatible bed mates, and a few days later at Babs' request she was moved down the veranda and her bed placed next to Ruth, who would chat idly with her for hours and share her passion for films.

Her parents visited every week, Nellie pushing Harry down the ward in a wheelchair, leaving the shop closed for the afternoon for the first time in its history. Their concern for their beloved daughter was obvious to see, and Babs milked it for all it was worth.

Babs made a good and speedy recovery from Tuberculosis and left the Sanatorium within a year. She eventually married a local boy whose village accent was strong with the south Derbyshire dialect that her mother had so disliked, but he adored Babs, and she was happy. On her parents' deaths she took over the village shop, and despite her 'posh' voice was successful, turning it into the district's first ever self-service.

A Taste of Freedom

When Dr Paul did the first of his New Year rounds, both Babs and I were given our long awaited two hours up. We were jubilant and out of our beds the minute he left the ward, skipping around the veranda, finding it difficult not to show our elation too obviously. We were very aware that other patients were still on bed rest and feeling that yet another month had passed them by with no progress made, but despite these feelings they all smiled and cheered, sharing in our delight.

At long last I felt a sense of hope and could now look forward to the future ahead. Over the past year, I had accepted that recovery from this illness would be a long, drawn out procedure, and not the quick cure that I had first expected. But whilst I had witnessed many deaths, my youthful optimism had never acknowledged that I too might not recover.

The first month of our allotted hours had to be spent on the ward. We were supposed to sit sedately in a chair next to our beds, with an occasional genteel stroll across the veranda to allow our weakened limbs to strengthen. But we two flitted madly from bed to bed, socialising with our bed-resting friends, endlessly filling their hot water bottles and winding long skeins of wool for the manic knitters of the ward. We even ventured into the kitchen to make everyone a cup of tea, but only on Sister McIvor's day off, the domestic quarters being strictly forbidden to patients.

At the end of the month if we were well and our daily progress good, we would be allowed to take the next big step. We could arrange to have our clothes brought in and take a daily gentle walk through the wooded grounds of the Sanatorium, warmly clad, and weather permitting of course.

How strange it was to wear underwear again – I fumbled when fastening the thick wool stockings to my first ever suspender belt which I had persuaded my mother to buy, not wanting the indignity of ankle socks. I had dearly wanted a bra, but was too embarrassed to ask for one. I was dismayed to find my old school skirt packed in the bag of clothes my mother had sent. I was sure Babs would be dressed in the height of fashion, making me look childish. Sure enough, my navy blue school coat was neatly folded at the bottom of the bag. I was only grateful that my soft Panama hat with the school badge on the front had not been included. I was comforted to see Babs wearing an equally shabby coat, and even had a few seconds of bliss when I saw her white ankle socks. This quickly faded when she pulled on a pair of new beautiful suede knee length boots and, whilst pulling up the long zips, gave a sideways smug look at my sensible laced brogues.

When we came out of the bathroom, both fully dressed for the first time in twelve months, everyone cheered and wolf whistled. It all felt very strange – it had seemed normal to be in pyjamas and now dressed, I was feeling out of place on the veranda, isolated from my friends who were still in bed. I wanted to tear off my clothes and re-join their safe, cosy group. But instead Babs and I donned our coats and the warm woolly hats that Janet, with this day in mind, had kindly knitted for us, and with one last wistful look at the beds we ventured timidly out through the main entrance of Ward B. We left behind calls of "Don't do anything I wouldn't do," and "Don't talk to strange men."

"If you do, bring them back here," Angie added.

We walked around the grounds that first day, calm and sedate as instructed, both of us in truth very nervous. We soon tired and after a mere ten minutes of the bracing air, we returned to the security of the veranda, clutching a few snowdrops, the only trophy of our outing. Over the next few days we became braver and brisker in our walking, and by the second week had grown a little bored with the monotony and scope of our daily strolls. The Sanatorium grounds, although pleasant enough, offered no adventure for two fifteen year olds and our walks seemed tedious.

Being of an inquiring nature and possibly more foolhardy than Babs, I suggested we should go further on our next venture out. On previous walks I had noticed a small gate behind the mortuary which seemed to give access to the other side of the hill and, ever curious, I wanted to explore it and widen our horizons. Bribing Babs with the loan of my suspender belt and stockings I convinced her to accompany me. We hurried past the mortuary, our eyes tightly closed, not wanting to even see the darkened windows or imagine what might be inside. We climbed over the gate and found ourselves at last in new and unknown territory.

The views were breathtaking, with miles of open countryside stretching out in front of us, the vista so clear it was difficult to see where sky and earth touched. We were both overcome with a sense of freedom and, grabbing hands, we danced down the hillside singing at the top of our voices. Eventually tiring, we stopped to rest in a small shady clump of trees. Babs, more prudent than I, wanted to go back. I reluctantly agreed and we turned our heads to look up the hill, which now with our sudden fatigue seemed a monstrous climb. Taking deep breaths we prepared to tackle it, and then to our dismay found we couldn't move; our feet were firmly stuck fast in a quagmire of thick mud, and to our horror we could feel the squelching sludge pulling us even deeper into the boggy marshland that we had chosen for our resting place.

It was getting dark and chilly, the bright day suddenly changing, as often happens in late winter. Babs started to cry and although at first I had found our predicament amusing, I too began to feel apprehensive. However, I quickly realised Babs' tears were not caused by alarm at our plight, but by the sudden realisation of the damage being inflicted on her new suede boots. Their fur trimmed tops were, by this time, the only visible sign left of their former glory. I tried to pull her free, but only succeeded in entrenching us both deeper.

"Help! Help! Please somebody, help!" we called in vain, the Sanatorium being out of earshot and a distant isolated cottage looking derelict and deserted. With a desperate effort, I managed to pull a foot free and by hauling myself on to an overhanging branch was able to get the other one clear. My socks were wet and dirty and my shoes had totally disappeared into the foul smelly sludge. I called to Babs to do the same, but she was alternating between weeping, calling for help, or reproaching me for enticing her to this horrid spot.

I accepted the blame and said I would go and look for assistance. Leaving her still stuck in the mud, snivelling and bemoaning the state of her boots, I cautiously made my way around the boggy land and, muddy and shoeless, stumbled out in to the darkness. Within seconds I had tripped and was rolling headfirst down the soggy grass bank, finally stopping next to a stone wall at the bottom of the hill. I was slightly dazed, bruised, breathless and very dirty, but managed to scramble to my feet and stagger the few yards needed to reach the secluded cottage we had seen from the top of the hill.

I banged on the door, sobbing, by now somewhat hysterical. No one answered, but I was sure the curtains had twitched and a glimmer of light briefly shown. I renewed my frenzied knocking – at last the porch light came on and the door opened, just wide enough for the double-barrelled shotgun that was thrust through the gap.

The gruff voice that came from the darkness behind the gun told me to go away or else! I turned and fled. The rough surface of the farm track that I was running down had cut my feet and blood was seeping through my muddy socks, but still I ran on, fearful that the gunman was close behind.

At last, winded and quite distraught I collapsed on the grass verge and wept. I was desperately worried about Babs, still stuck in the bog, imagining her by now almost submerged, with perhaps just a few blonde curls showing on top of the bubbling mud. And then, even more alarming, my thoughts turned to Sister McIvor, whose anger would be turned on me if I returned to the ward alone. Wiping my tears with a grubby sleeve, I limped on, not knowing where the track led, but putting as much distance as I could manage between my dejected figure and that gun.

A flickering light was slowly approaching along the bumpy lane in front of me, and I gave a huge sigh of relief when I saw the uniformed man astride an old squeaky push bike. "I think you must be the little lass I'm looking for," he said, and propping me up on his crossbar turned and slowly peddled back the mile or so to his police house, where warmly wrapped in his cloak and sipping a mug of cocoa I told him my sorry tale.

"Don't worry yourself about the other lassie. She's safe, and in a better state than you," he said, "and old Tom at the cottage was probably terrified seeing your desperate face at his door. He's a bit eccentric, but harmless, and he doesn't encourage visitors."

I was collected from the police house by the porter, driving the Sanatorium van. He told me that there had been a real panic on the ward when Babs and I had not returned for tea. Sister McIvor had sent him and the gardener to search the grounds for us, not thinking we would have dared disobey her orders and gone further afield. "Luckily," he said, we had been seen climbing over the gate by the mortuary cleaner. Babs had been quickly found and rescued from her muddy snare, and she had soon been tucked up in bed; and found to be none the worse for her ordeal. Unsure of which direction I had taken, Sister McIvor had rung the police and reported me missing.

I was furious – whilst I was being held at gunpoint, cutting my feet to shreds, and rolling down hills in a valiant attempt to save her, Babs had been in bed having tea and sympathy.

Arriving back and pushed on to the ward in a wheelchair, I was met by gasps of shock and horror; my bruised and battered appearance looking far worse than it really was. Bathed and bandaged, I was put to bed, and Sister McIvor drew the screens tightly around me, as if she thought I might contaminate the other patients. Concealed in disgrace I could hear the outpourings of condolences given to Babs over the sad loss of her precious boots. No one cared about the loss of my one and only pair of stockings.

A Little Holiday (Nan's Story)

It was no surprise to Nancy when she found herself pregnant for the fifth time in as many years. She had married Terry on her seventeenth birthday, already six months gone with her first. Beryl, her mother, had begged her not to marry him. Despite the shame of her daughter having an illegitimate baby she was adamant, not wanting her to make the mistake she had made herself eighteen years earlier, when she had married Nancy's father for the same reason.

Admittedly, Terry Parsons was a good looking lad who could, if he wanted, charm the birds out of the trees, but he was work shy and liked his beer too much, and that to Nancy's mum didn't make for good husband material. Still, Nancy, or Nan as she liked to be called, went ahead and married him. Afterwards people gossiped about her early confinement, but all agreed that at least he'd done the decent thing and wed her. Beryl sadly shook her head, and uttered the well-worn adage, "She's made her bed, and now she will have to lie on it."

And lie on it she did, enduring Terry's alcohol fuelled passion every night for the next five years. Repeated pregnancies had taken a toll on her girlish good looks. At twenty-two years of age she was careworn, permanently tired, and utterly sick of Terry. After the difficult birth of her fifth child she had taken a long time to recover, and the doctor had told her, "No more children Mrs Parsons, you have your hands full already."

"Try telling that to Terry," she muttered under her breath.

The first year of their marriage they had lived with Mrs Parsons senior, sharing the single bed in Terry's bedroom. His mother had disliked Nan at first sight, thinking she had taken advantage of her good-natured son, and repeatedly told her so. She constantly criticised Nan's parenting skills, mocking her finicky ways, considering her too fussy in the care of her new born son. Nan, in desperation, found a small cottage to rent. It was dark and dingy, and situated in a mean back street, but it was hers. She persuaded her reluctant husband to leave his mother and start their married life anew in their own place. They begged and borrowed enough furniture and household goods to enable them to set up home. In spite of Nan's best efforts, the little house remained damp and bug ridden, but the rent was cheap, and Terry was never in work long enough to allow them to afford anything better.

Despite their poor living conditions, she kept her children clean and healthy, feeding them as well as she could on the limited housekeeping that Terry allowed her, often going without food herself to ensure that they had enough to eat. Terry would flit between the pub and his mother's, where his charm could always get him a meal and a few shillings to buy another drink.

Beryl was worried about her daughter's health, concerned at her haggard appearance. Before her marriage Nan had been a fresh faced, robust girl, and now she was a shadow of her former self, a pale, scrawny figure, her once glossy auburn hair thin and dull. During the bitterly cold winter months she had developed a dull ache in her chest, and eventually her exhaustion was so intense she could no longer cope.

Terry had risen at midday, having overslept after a particularly heavy drinking session at the Rose & Crown the night before. He was shocked to find no fire in the grate, no food on the table, the children hungry and still in their pyjamas, the new baby wet and fretful whimpering in his pram, and most shocking of all – his wife asleep on the shabby couch, oblivious of the chaos around her. On closer inspection he could see that she was bathed in sweat, and her breathing was shallow and laboured.

Hurriedly he pulled on his trousers and shoes, fastening his shirt as he ran through the back streets to his mother-in-law's house, where he gasped out his fears. Beryl, not stopping to change her slippers, raced back with him, her heart pounding with panic and exertion as she tried to keep up with Terry's frantic pace. As they ran she angrily berated him for his feckless ways, her worry making her more blunt than usual.

One glance at the flushed, prostrated figure on the couch was enough to convince her that it was a doctor that was needed, and Terry was sharply told to make haste and find one before his wife got worse. Nan was taken to the local infirmary where she was found to be suffering from pleurisy. The doctors told Terry that she was in such a weakened state they feared she might not last the night. Her lack of nourishment and physical weakness had contributed in making her seriously ill.

He panicked, imagining the disturbance and turmoil that would enter his life if she died. "I can't look after five kids on my own," he said. Beryl looked at him in disgust. She was sitting at Nan's bedside holding her frail hands, trying to pass on some of her own strength and energy to the sick girl.

Nan survived the night, but later, after a more thorough examination and x-rays she was diagnosed with Pulmonary Tuberculosis. Her mother took the children back home to stay with her, and Nan was taken to the Sanatorium. Terry, true to form, drowned his sorrows in the Rose & Crown.

When Nan first arrived on Ward B she was too ill to realise where she was or notice her fellow patients, but after a few days of complete bed rest and regular meals she started to feel better and take note of her surroundings. She had no idea of what ailed her, and couldn't understand why she was in a Sanatorium. She had felt too ill and mentally remote to take notice of what the doctors had told her.

Nan loved Ward B. She said it was like waking every morning to find yourself in heaven. To be able to lie for twenty-four hours a day in a warm bed, having food and drink brought to you, was wonderful. She worried about her babies and missed them, but was reassured to know that they were with her mother, who with the help of Nan's aunt, was taking good care of them. She never even thought of Terry, but just had a feeling of great relief that he was not there. She relished the peaceful nights in a comfortable bed where she could be alone without his drunken groping.

Nan blossomed on the veranda, regaining some of her youthful looks and exuberance. She enjoyed the company of the other women, and captured some of the enthusiasm for life that she had lost during the daily struggle of her unfortunate marriage. She always said that her stay on Ward B was the best holiday she'd ever had.

Nan was a patient on the ward for a year. Whilst she was away Terry had returned to live with his mother, and was soon enjoying his bachelor status again. He rarely visited his wife or enquired about the children. By the time Nan was ready for home leave, he had moved a young pregnant girlfriend into his mother's spare bedroom, and had almost forgotten the results of his past folly.

Terry would never change. His heavy drinking soon marred his good looks, and the children from his and Nan's ill-fated marriage shunned him. He died lonely in middle age from Cirrhosis of the liver.

On her release from the Sanatorium Nan and her children were allocated a new council house. She was able to bring up her family in a pleasant and happier environment, and when her youngest started school Nan returned to the Sanatorium to train as a nurse. She had a successful career, put all her children through higher education, and is now a much loved, proud and happy grandmother.

She never had another man in her life. Once was enough she said.

41

An Afternoon Matinee

After our previous misadventure Babs had kept her distance, pointedly walking in the opposite direction whenever she saw me in the grounds. She was still bitter about the loss of her precious boots, which although retrieved by the gardener, were found to be utterly ruined. This huge loss she laid firmly at my door, and I had become the scapegoat of the whole disastrous affair. She cheered up a little when her doting parents bought her some new ones the following weekend, but continued to eye me with deep suspicion.

Babs was an avid film fan, and before entering the Sanatorium had visited the cinema at least twice a week. She was knowledgeable about all the Hollywood stars, gaining most of her information from the 'Picturegoer' magazine. She loved to gossip about their love affairs, and the beautiful mansions where they held their glitzy parties. She always spoke as if she was their personal friend. Her proudest possession was an album of glossy black and white studio photographs of all her favourite stars, the most important being the one bearing the hand-written message – 'To Babs, my best regards, Gregory Peck,' followed by two large XXs. He was her heart throb, and she prayed every night that she would be given home leave in time to see his latest film.

A few weeks after she had expressed this desire I noted, whilst scanning the local newspaper, that the Ritz Cinema was proudly presenting 'Roman Holiday' starring Gregory Peck – the very film she was so anxious to see. The advertisement stated that it was to be shown for three days only, and the very next day would be the final performance.

Being devious minded I kept this information to myself, but later that night when helping Babs fill hot water bottles I chose to whisper my secret to her. She was very excited, and after allowing her time to ponder the information, I casually said "Shall we go?" She reared back from me in shock, but I could see that my mischievous idea had taken root. We had both recently been given an extra hour, and we were now allowed three hours up, but had been banned from leaving the Sanatorium grounds; our last escapade causing enough grief as far as

Sister McIvor was concerned. Our daily walks had become very tedious, and the initial excitement of being dressed and free to leave the confines of the ward had long ago lost its appeal.

I was not surprised the next morning when Babs, passing my bed, whispered the word "YES" and nodded me towards the bathroom. Her love of the cinema had overcome her prudence and her distrust of my foolish ideas. We made our plans, and once lunch and the rest period were over, we hastily dressed and left the ward separately, not wanting to raise suspicious thoughts about our sudden chumminess.

Meeting in the bushes alongside the tall iron gates we waited for the porter to leave his lodge. He always went up to Ward A at this time for a cup of tea and a chat with one of the nurses he fancied. Our daily walks in the grounds had not been wasted. We knew everyone's routines, and all their little secrets. Sure enough, he came out on time, and as we suspected headed straight to the men's ward. We then simply pushed the gates open and brazenly walked out of the grounds without a backward glance.

It was a pleasant afternoon, and early spring sunshine warmed our backs as we briskly walked down the hill. At the bottom, we found a bus about to leave for town. Sitting on the top deck we surveyed the passing scenery without a care in the world. It was such a wonderful feeling to be free of the Sanatorium, and going to the pictures just like anybody else our age. I would have sat there all afternoon, daydreaming, and simply enjoying the bus ride, but Babs, anxious to reach the cinema, pulled me downstairs and off the bus when the town centre was reached.

She was disappointed when we arrived at the cinema to find that "Roman Holiday" had been given an A certificate, barring us from seeing the film without an accompanying adult. We were both only fifteen, and looked even younger in our school coats. I felt relieved, having had second thoughts about our little adventure since arriving in town. The bustling crowded pavements, and the noise of passing traffic was making me feel flustered and uneasy – I wanted to be back on the veranda, where everything was familiar and safe.

But Babs had no intention of missing Gregory Peck, and showing a surprising bossy streak, pushed me to the front of the cinema and started to ask adults in the queue if they would accompany us in. Cringing with embarrassment I pretended to look at the film scenes portrayed in the glass fronted bill boards, but Babs had quickly found an elderly couple who, charmed by her sweet smile and good manners, agreed to take us in. Grabbing my arm, she marched me up to the box office behind her new found friends. Within minutes we were seated in the back stalls watching the end of the Movietone News with the big picture still to come.

Babs was enthralled, staring fixedly at the screen, but I felt uncomfortable, and ill at ease. The smoky atmosphere was tickling my throat, and I developed an irritating cough which caused some tut-tutting from the seats behind me. Babs' remedy was to pinch me hard every time it happened, annoyed at the interruptions to her enjoyment of Gregory Peck.

Much to my relief the film ended and it was time to leave, but Babs was furious with me for refusing to stay on in our seats to watch it come round again. We left the cinema in silence, walking through separate doors, but meeting on the steps, we both blinked at the sudden light which was confusing after the darkness of the cinema.

The chiming of the nearby town hall clock made us recollect that we only had twenty minutes left, and we should by now be back on the ward, preparing to undress and take to our beds again.

We were unsure of where our return bus departed from, and belatedly realised that we didn't know its destination either. Babs, chatting excitedly about the film seemed to have no thoughts of our dilemma, and was even suggesting we could repeat the venture the following week, her appetite now whetted by the lengthy film trailers she had just seen. By contrast I was slowly beginning to realise what a stupid idea the whole outing had been.

We found the bus station, and inquired about buses that would take us to the bottom of the hill below the Sanatorium. "No more tonight," the inspector told us. "There's only three round trips a day on that route." We stared at him in dismay. It had never crossed our minds that we would be unable to get back in time for tea.

After asking for directions we set off to walk, not realising it was all of five miles. Following the main road out of town we somehow took a wrong turning, finding ourselves on a large suburban estate. It was like a maze, with endless cul-de-sacs that led us nowhere. We were both by now weary, and feeling the effects of our additional exertions. We were shivering, our coats no longer so warm as an evening chill crept in. The sky was darkening, and the street lights suddenly came on, illuminating our way, but offering no warmth or comfort.

We felt very alone, and both missed the safety of the veranda and our friends. As we walked on past the rows of terraced houses, we saw glimpses through open curtains of cosy interiors, families sitting in front of roaring fires listening to the wireless, small children sipping hot drinks warmly wrapped in their dressing gowns, and how we envied the people who were sat at dining tables having their evening meal. We were both hungry, not having eaten since our early lunch, and we were glad that some had tightly drawn their curtains, blocking such domestic bliss from our view. The bright lights became further apart as we left the urban streets behind, and the houses became more spacious with larger gardens. The occasional dim street lights were throwing threatening shadows in our path. Then it started to rain, and soon we were walking with wet feet and dripping hair.

Babs sat on a garden wall and burst into tears. "I can't walk any more," she said. Feeling responsible for her distress I put my arms round her, sat next to her on the wall and cried too.

The front door of a nearby house suddenly opened, its hall light shining on our tear stained faces. A young woman came out and asked if she could help. We explained our predicament, and asked if we could shelter and rest for a while. She was kindly and caring, until we mentioned that we were patients at the Sanatorium. At this disclosure she changed, and a look of fear crossed her face. "I'm sorry," she said, "but I can't ask you in. I have two young children to think about." And with that she slammed the door.

In those few minutes of light, I had seen how pale and drained Babs looked, and for the first time felt panic, worried that we both might collapse in the hedge bottom, and die before morning.

We had only struggled a little way up the street before a delicious smell of fish and chips wafted towards us. With renewed energy we broke into a run, and on turning the next corner saw the steamy windows of a chip shop. By pooling our money we had just enough for cod and chips twice, and a bottle of ginger beer. Food had never tasted so good. Ten minutes later, when licking our greasy fingers and sharing the last drop of ginger beer, we faced the truth – we were now one hour late, and hopelessly lost.

Feeling more cheered by the hot food we plodded on, hopeful of soon finding the right road. It was much later, whilst resting on a bench by the side of a lit phone box that I had an idea. Turning to Babs, who was whimpering, having just discovered a blister on her heel I said, "Don't worry about that. I've just had a brilliant idea."

"Oh no, not another one!" she groaned, and stood up to walk away.

"No, wait," I called out to her. "Come back and listen. Why don't we ring the emergency number? The way I see it, we are already patients, and live in a hospital, and this is a real emergency. Why not call an ambulance?"

Without waiting for an answer, I entered the phone box and dialled 999.

Babs joined me, and we stood close together inside, sheltering from the driving rain, waiting to be rescued. The box stank of stale cigarettes and urine, and catching a glimpse of my face in the tiny mirror above the phone I was shocked. The reflection showed flushed cheeks, eyes too bright, and a strange wildness in my expression.

At last with its bell clanging the ambulance arrived. No questions were asked. One look at our damp, distraught state was enough. Bundled in blankets, we were driven back through the big iron gates that only a few hours earlier we had so confidently walked out of.

Sister McIvor and Staff Nurse Levy were waiting on the ward steps as we were both carried in. Not a word was spoken. We were quickly stripped of our wet clothing, and put straight to bed in the small side ward next to Sister McIvor's office. She had already sternly warned the other patients to keep their distance. They were disappointed, all longing to know what mischief we had been up to this time. After sipping hot milk and swallowing a sleeping tablet, I drifted blissfully off to sleep, groggily registering surprise when Sister McIvor smoothed back my hair, and lightly kissed me on the forehead. Later when thinking about it, I assumed I must have been hallucinating at the time.

We both developed heavy colds, and were kept in the side ward for two weeks on complete bed rest. Luckily neither of us suffered any lasting damage, and when put back into our permanent beds on the veranda, felt we had at last come home.

Once we were fully recovered Sister McIvor invited us both into her office for a wee chat. Her delicate way of putting it didn't deceive us. We knew that it was lecture time. She firmly clicked the door behind us, something she rarely did, so we guessed it was going to be serious. She looked at us both with sadness, and not anger, which scared us even more. "I'm really very disappointed in you both," she said. "You two girls are amongst the lucky ones. You have gained your hours, and are regaining your health, but your stupidity put all this in jeopardy, and caused immense worry to staff and your fellow patients. That was very thoughtless. You both know that there are people on this ward who will never reach the privileges that you so foolishly abused."

We hung our heads in shame. Babs started to say that it had all been my fault, but Sister McIvor stopped her, and said, "If this juvenile behaviour continues I shall send you both to the children's ward, where you perhaps more appropriately belong." Tearful and thoroughly chastened, we returned to the veranda.

When Dr Paul did his next round, I was mortified when, walking away from my bed, he turned back and asked if I had enjoyed my Roman Holiday, winking at me as he said it.

"Yes," I replied, blushing crimson.

Sister McIvor gave me one of her looks, and then thankfully they all moved on.

The Spoils of War (Elsa's Story)

She would have a nightmare at least once a week, waking us all up in fright when she repeatedly screamed and shouted out, using a language we didn't understand. Eileen or Nan would help Night Sister hold her still until she had calmed down. The next morning her apologies would be profuse.

"Pardon, I beg of you all. Bitte, bitte, please forgive me."

Elsa was a pretty girl, a natural blonde with a lovely luminous complexion. She had deep set pale blue eyes that always had heavy dark shadows under-lining them. Her soft voice was difficult to understand, a guttural German accent overriding her attempts to speak English. She was very ill when first carried into the small room next to Sister McIvor's office – we could hear her laboured breathing and endless bouts of coughing. But she improved and soon joined us on the veranda.

She was the first real German any of us had seen, and with the war still fresh in our memories we half expected her to say, "Heil Hitler" and jump to attention when spoken to. But Elsa's sweet nature and her quiet manner soon ridiculed those foolish thoughts. Over the next few months she told us her story, omitting much that she feared might distress us. We heard enough to realise that, whatever the outcome of war, it's innocent people on all sides who suffer.

The small Prussian village where Elsa was born no longer exists. It disappeared off the map after the Russians swept through it, in their race to reach Berlin in the final days of the Second World War. Her family had farmed there for generations, and were fiercely proud of their Prussian heritage, considering themselves the true Germans. Elsa was the eldest of three girls, with one elder brother, Erich, who at this crucial time was, like their father, lost somewhere in the white wastes of Russia with the defeated Germany army.

She was just sixteen years of age when the church bells rang out their warning, a pre-arranged signal to alert the villagers of danger. She ran with everyone else to the church, where the priest told them that the Russians were only a few kilometres away. They had all seen the hordes of refugees passing through their village, and heard the horror stories of the advancing army's cruelty, the wanton destruction of life and land. Now it was their turn to flee.

Elsa had returned home to find her mother already packing provisions, and after feeding the farm animals and turning them loose, she dressed herself and her sisters in their warmest clothes. Their grandmother, who was in bad health, begged them to go and leave her behind. She said she would die in her own bed, and was not afraid. Putting food and water within her reach, and with the sounds of gunfire drawing nearer, they all hastily embraced the old lady and left, there being no time for sentiment.

Pushing a small handcart loaded with a few snatched possessions, Elsa, her mother, and two little sisters joined the exodus from the only life they had ever known. Elsa had never thought of leaving the village – she had expected to marry one of the local boys and have children, who would grow up to follow the traditions of their farming ancestors. At the first bend in the road she stopped, and turned to look back at her home. Framed by the rising sun it looked so normal, smoke still curling from its chimneys. She couldn't believe she might never see it again. Taking a pebble from the road as a keepsake, she turned away from the village, and tightly gripping her young sister's hand resolutely followed in her mother's footsteps.

It was a sad stream of people, rich and poor alike, who trudged westward hoping to find safety and shelter. Their numbers swelled as they walked on, many other village communities also fleeing the unknown terror. After three days of walking Elsa's family, despite their meagre portions, had used all their provisions. They chewed grass and sucked on small stones to ease their hunger pangs, their thoughts only of food. As Elsa's feet stumbled forward of their own accord she tortured herself with memories of her mother's kitchen, the spicy sausages hanging from the rafters, a tasty stew bubbling on the range, and the delicious smell of freshly baked bread. She could almost taste a warm crusty chunk, thickly spread with their own churned butter that would melt in her mouth.

The sudden roar of a plane bought her back to the present. Without any warning a hail of bullets rained down. The refugees scattered into ditches or where ever they could find shelter. The Russian plane continued to harass them, swooping in low and shooting indiscriminately. Elsa's younger sister was hit. She died without a sound as they lifted her down from her mother's back.

She was gently laid under a tree and left there alone whilst her family walked on, numb with grief, the silent tears frozen on their faces. Ever watchful for the attacking planes they snatched brief periods of sleep, the early winter frosts chilling their bodies as they lay huddled together in hedge bottoms, or inside an occasional empty barn. Elsa saw many people lie down on the roadside, simply too exhausted to go on. Old people died, and babies were born, but still they plodded onwards, afraid to stay too long in any place, knowing the Russians were not far behind.

Time no longer seemed important. They were unaware that they had been walking for almost two weeks, living off the already scavenged land, eating roots and wild berries, drinking water from the fetid ditches that ran alongside their track. Most of the refugees were suffering from diarrhoea and were using the same ditches for their necessary repeated stops.

Every step for Elsa had become agony. Her feet were blistered and bleeding, but when her sharp eyes spotted a small crop of potatoes that others had overlooked, she left her mother's side and ran across the field, tearing out the frozen plants, cramming the raw half grown potatoes in her mouth, chewing them with relish, dirt and all. The next day they reached a railway junction. Here they were allowed to board an empty freight train that was also speeding west trying to flee the Russian advance.

Two weeks after leaving their home, Elsa, her mother, and sister arrived at a transit camp on the outskirts of Berlin. Along with thousands of other refugees, they were given shelter in a crumbling abandoned abattoir. There was no sanitation, water or food. A soup kitchen was organised by local nuns, but there was never enough for everyone.

The tragic loss of her youngest daughter and the long trek had taken its toll of Elsa's mother. She seemed to have lost her will to live, relying on her eldest daughter for guidance and support. Elsa went out every day searching the bombed suburbs of Berlin for food or saleable goods. On one of these forages she discovered an unoccupied cellar, the elegant building above it long since gone, a victim of Allied bombing. The cellar was secure and dry, and by exploring the ruins of similar properties she gathered together a collection of broken furniture, abandoned pots and pans, and a large amount of wood.

Elsa fetched her mother and sister from the camp. They took possession of their new home, and later that evening when sitting on rickety chairs in front of a blazing wood fire eating the windfall apples found in the orchard behind the cellar, they almost felt a sense of happiness.

They felt safe, never imagining that Berlin could fall. Now their most pressing need was money to buy food. Early the next morning

Elsa took her mother's gold wedding ring to barter on the street market. She found money was no longer of any use, and exchanged it instead for a loaf of black bread and two small onions. Feeling uneasy with so many hungry eyes watching her movements, she hid the precious bargains under her coat and made her way back through the ruins to the cellar.

She was almost there, when a rough hand was clamped across her mouth and she was dragged into a half-ruined basement where, throwing her to the ground, her assailant brutally raped her. He took the bread and onions, leaving her bruised and sobbing on the dirty floor. She crawled back to the cellar where her mother was as shocked by her appearance as by the loss of the bartered goods. Elsa told her she had tripped on the rubble and dropped the food into a crevice as she fell. Her mother cried, and Elsa with her, but there was no time to weep or mourn her lost innocence. She had to find a way to feed them all.

But then the Russians came – *Elsa would weep when she came to this part of her story, shaking her head and saying she could never tell us about that time. It was too horrible.*

Later she enlisted in a gang of refugees who were clearing the roads of rubble. It was hard and dangerous work with unexploded bombs amongst the debris. Her hands were torn and bleeding, but she carried on, knowing she would receive bread, and perhaps some sausage to take back to the family. As the roads were cleared she worked further away from the cellar, and one day she excitedly headed home clutching the two small eggs she had been given, such a treat for her mother and sister.

She found her way blocked, a barricade across the road, and Russian soldiers patrolling it. She discovered that her family were now residents of a newly formed Russian zone, and she was left in the British sector alone. The politics of Germany's defeat had passed them by, their main concerns having been food and shelter. She screamed and shouted her mother's name, but to no avail. She sat in sight of the barricade all night hoping for a glimpse of her mother and sister, knowing they would be frantic with worry at her absence. Her vigil produced no miracles. She never saw either of them again.

Elsa lost her mind for a while, but her determination to survive was strong. She cleared roads by day and drifted from cellar to cellar by night. She became one of a group of young displaced people who clung together like flotsam, and whose lives seemed to have no meaning any more. They found a partially damaged apartment which had survived the collapse of its adjacent buildings, and despite its lack of doors and floorboards gave them a more permanent home.

Elsa obtained work in a cement factory producing concrete slabs which were in great demand for re-building the devastated city. For the first time she was receiving a wage, and was able to purchase some second-hand shoes, having worn a pair of over-large men's boots for many months. With better food available in the British sector she was feeling almost human again, but was still grieving for her lost family.

Hurrying home to the apartment one night, lowering her head against the sleet, she slipped, almost falling under the wheels of a British Army jeep. The driver stopped, jumping out to ask if she was alright. She didn't understand what he was saying, but was grateful for his concern and smiled back her thanks. The next night the jeep was parked on the same stretch of road, the driver leaning against it waiting for her – with no grasp of his words she quickly recognised the jar of coffee he held out to her.

After this he was waiting for her every night as she came home from work. He was a shy, lonely young British soldier who had felt warmed by her smile. He was very respectful, and she introduced him to her friends who were impressed by his good manners, and more so by his gifts of chocolate and cigarettes. They were like gold on the black market.

When Joe's superior officers discovered he had a German girlfriend he was taken off patrols and confined to camp. Elsa missed him, and not just for his valuable gifts. She had grown to respect the quiet gentle Englishman; he was kind and thoughtful, virtues that had been sadly lacking in her life since leaving the village.

Joe wrote and asked her to marry him and she said yes. They were married six weeks later by a sympathetic army padre. Joe was immediately shipped back to England, marriage to a German girl unpopular with the authorities. It took him a year to cut through the red tape to allow his bride to follow.

Joe took her home to Staffordshire to meet his family. She was shy and afraid when arriving at their home. He pushed her forward and proudly introduced her to his waiting relatives. After a long silence in which Elsa was studied from head to toe, Joe's mother said, "I don't want a German in my house. She's not welcome here." Elsa had no understanding of the words, but realised from the angry gestures that she was being rejected. The war had left many British women bereft of sons and husbands, and at that time German brides were not welcomed.

When Joe was demobbed a few weeks later, they started their married life. They rented a small, two roomed basement flat. It was dark and damp, with a permanent musty smell, but Elsa was very happy. She cleaned and scrubbed the dingy rooms, and cooked delicious meals for her Joe.

She was always slender and as time passed became painfully thin. Joe worried about her constant tiredness, and the chronic irritating cough that she said was a legacy of the cement works and her years of deprivation. But she agreed to see a doctor to appease Joe's anxiety. They were told she had advanced Tuberculosis. She cried bitter tears, weeping for the family and life she had lost, and now she had to leave her Joe.

The following day Elsa entered the Sanatorium.

We had no words to express our feelings when she told us these grim facts of her past life. She would tell us a little each night, and as we lay in the darkness listening to her we all felt her pain. The veranda would be silent as she wept, but one of us would get out of bed and go to her, holding her tight, hoping we could convey the compassion we couldn't articulate.

Her Joe would come each visiting day, clasping her frail hands in both of his, as if willing his own strength to her. His love was obvious to see, although her brave ex-soldier would blush to the roots of his fiery red hair when she passionately kissed him before he left.

We all willed her to get well too. We couldn't bear the thought of Elsa losing her new-found happiness. It just wouldn't be fair.

Elsa did recover. It took three years before she was able to go back to her Joe. They had forty very happy years together, both working hard to buy their own home, and delighted when a daughter arrived whom they called Anja, which had been Elsa's mother's name.

In 1989 when the Berlin wall was dismantled, Elsa registered with the Red Cross hoping to find some trace of her family. A few months later she was contacted by her brother Erich who had been living in East Germany since his release from a Russian labour camp. The two of them had an emotional meeting the following year, when Elsa flew to Berlin to be reunited with the only other member of her family to survive. She lost her Joe a few years later when he died of a sudden heart attack. But she is still living in the little house they shared, surrounded by her grandchildren, feeling blessed to have had such a long and happy life.

Duty Calls (Sister McIvor's Story)

Sister McIvor's family had a long and distinguished history of military service. Over the years McIvor men had given their allegiance, and in some cases their lives in every corner of the world, their name being acclaimed on numerous regimental rolls of honour. It was no surprise when young Jean McIvor opted to join the prestigious Queen Alexandra's Royal Nursing Corps – she was simply continuing the family tradition.

She had been born at her grandparents' home in Edinburgh, just six months to the day that her father, Captain Alistair McIvor, had sacrificed his life for king and country – killed by a sniper's bullet when he foolishly raised his head above a trench in the latter days of the First World War. Jean's birth had been a bitter disappointment; her mother and paternal grandparents had hoped for a boy, to uphold the family name and its proud military record.

She had grown up a lonely child in the dark gloomy terraced house that lay in the shadow of the famous castle. Her mother had become a self-imposed invalid after the untimely death of her beloved husband, and other than an occasional afternoon's drive in the family carriage she never left her room, feeling far too delicate to cope with a child. The elderly grandparents were of the generation that believed children should be rarely seen, and never heard.

The little girl's nursery was on the upper floor of the house well away from the adults, its cupboards still full of her father's childhood toys. She had found a box of his well-used lead soldiers, and spent many solitary hours lining up the colourful little armies to fight imaginary battles. She was occasionally joined by old Hamish who would get down on his rheumaticky knees and help direct the line of fire.

Old Hamish had been her grandfather's batman, and had retired from service at the same time as his beloved Major. With no family of his own he had accepted the Major's offer to accompany him back to Scotland. He kept the garden tidy, and did all the household's odd jobs in return for his bed and board. He'd made himself comfortable in the basement and with his army pension was quite content, but still rose daily at 6 a.m. to polish the Major's boots and take up his morning tea – old habits hard to change.

He'd mourned young Alistair's death as deeply as the family had, and felt sorry for the little lassie, never knowing her father, having a mother who was over-occupied with her nerves, and grandparents too old and set in their ways to have patience with a wee bairn. She had a young Highland girl as nursemaid, but Hamish always tried to give her that extra bit of attention and companionship that he felt she lacked. Despite his gruff and grumpy exterior Jean was always able to touch his heart and bring a smile to his wrinkled face. As she grew older she followed him everywhere, patiently watching him do his tasks around the house, and digging her own little patch besides his in the garden. He escorted her to the small private school she attended, wiping away the tears on her first morning, and then standing proud and erect at the school gate each afternoon waiting to take her home again, butterscotch in his pocket, and a glass of milk and shortbread on the kitchen table ready for her return.

They would sit together in front of the kitchen range on cold winter evenings, and he would tell her stirring tales of past famous battles, describing the splendour of the magnificent regimental balls held in the officers' mess, with McIvor men in full dress uniform, swords at their sides, and the ladies in beautiful gowns with diamonds glinting in their ears as they twirled around the dance floor. The little girl's eyes glistened with excitement. She was enthralled by his stories, and unwittingly absorbed the legends and traditions of her family's past.

She found it hard leaving Hamish when her application to join the Royal Nursing Corps was accepted. The night before her departure she sat in the kitchen with the old man, both of them finding it difficult to say their goodbyes, he handing her a small tissue wrapped gift telling her to open it on the train the next day. Clearing his suddenly choked up throat he told her how pleased he was at her decision to nurse, and at her choice of such a prestigious nursing service. Taking hold of her hand and looking intently at her face, as if to store her features in his memory, he said, "Aye lassie, your father would have been as proud of you as I am."

Jean threw her arms round the old man, and promised that she would never let him or the McIvor name down. He looked away as she turned at the kitchen door to blow a final kiss, not wanting her to see his tears. Blowing his nose hard, he muttered angrily, "Och, maybe an old man will get a wee bit of peace now the pestering bairn's gone."

Jean opened the little tissue wrapped gift as the train left Edinburgh station. Inside was a shiny medal inscribed with the words 'Awarded to

Hamish Rose for outstanding valour and dedication to duty.' She cradled it gently in her hand, and quietly cried until the train had left the city far behind. Then she wiped her eyes, straightened her shoulders, and looked ahead to the future.

At the start of the Second World War she was already a qualified nurse, and had just completed her first tour of duty. In her early twenties, she was no beauty, but had a clean cut Celtic look with her father's sandy hair, and a pleasant open freckled face. Her eyes were steely blue and very direct, as was her speech. She didn't suffer fools or accept shoddy work, and her junior nurses were all a little afraid of her.

This was the Sister McIvor that Dr Michael Lawrence met and fell in love with. He was a respected surgeon working at the same field hospital as she in North Africa. They worked side by side under canvas, fighting against the blistering heat, sand, and the eternal flies, desperately trying to save the lives of the badly wounded young men that were bought in from battle, maimed and dying. The carnage made no sense to Jean, but she tirelessly and skilfully assisted the young doctor with his delicate surgery. Her steady hands and calm manner were invaluable to him. It was a strange setting for love to blossom, the smell of death always close by. But he grew to love and respect his quiet Scots nurse, seeing beauty in her lilting accent and trim figure, and most of all the honesty and sincerity that shone in her face. She returned his love, admiring his skill and dogged determination as he fought to save his patients' lives, and loving the warm smile that lit up his face when at the end of a difficult operation he showed his gratitude for her unfailing assistance.

It was no secret on the camp that they were in love, and everyone thought them well-suited – both having unshakeable values, and sharing the same ethics of work and unstinting service. They managed a magical weekend away together, visiting Cairo where they had chance for two short days to be happy young lovers. Michael bought her a silver embossed ring in a street market, and gave it to her as a token of his love. They knew that they wouldn't marry until the war was over, and were content with the snatched moments they had.

The heat and overwork was affecting Michael's health. Never robust, he was rapidly losing weight, and often had to stand back from his patients when a spasm of coughing overcame him, deep racking coughs that alarmed Jean. Dismayed as she was when he was sent home on sick leave, she was also very relieved that he would be in a cooler climate, and well away from the choking dust of the desert. They wrote long loving letters to each other, making plans for their future together after the war had ended. They shared a dream of running a small cottage hospital in the clean fresh air of the Scottish Highlands, and Jean, still working in the suffocating heat of the desert was impatient for these dreams to come true.

Sadly, Michael died of Pulmonary Tuberculosis two weeks before the end of the war. Jean was inconsolable, but true to her nature didn't show her grief. She left the nursing corps as soon as she was able, and went to Europe working with displaced people in refugee camps. She worked long hours, and the sick and destitute people she nursed helped to heal the savage pain in her own heart. These were people who had lost everything; in some cases their will to live. Her exhaustion and dedication saved her from despair. She knew instinctively that she would never marry or have another relationship. Her regard for Michael had been so deep she could never allow another man to challenge it.

She had only been back to Edinburgh twice since joining the nursing corps. The first time was to attend her grandfather's funeral, and the second a few weeks later when Hamish had died. The old soldier had been bereft without the Major that he had served so faithfully for six decades, and after walking behind his coffin and giving a last final salute he had returned to the basement and taken to his bed, where a few weeks later he'd died peacefully in his sleep. Her grandmother had died a few years earlier whilst Jean had been serving abroad, and her mother had long ago taken her fragile nerves to a nursing home in the south of England, where she resided happily with people of a similar disposition.

The gloomy house and its contents now belonged to Jean. She wandered through the empty rooms, not wanting any of its dusty relics, taking only the box of lead soldiers from the nursery, and an old framed photograph of herself and Hamish that she had found on his bedside table. She finally locked the door and after making arrangements for the house to be cleared and sold, left Scotland for ever.

Her 40th birthday in sight, she felt a growing need to settle in one place and put down some roots. She saw an advertisement in a nursing journal that appealed to her – an experienced nursing sister was required, to have sole responsibility for a busy female ward of a Staffordshire Sanatorium, a small cottage in the spacious grounds to be included. It seemed to be exactly what she needed. She had considerable experience, having nursed many tubercular patients in the refugee camps, and strong personal reasons for wanting to nurse the unfortunate victims of this devastating illness.

It had been a long and varied path that had brought Sister McIvor to Ward B. She spent the rest of her working life dedicated to helping the tubercular patients in her care. She was always deeply distressed when despite her best efforts she would lose one of her charges to the deadly bacteria, but her grieving was always done in the privacy of her cottage. She was a daunting figure, authoritative, strict, and fanatical about hygiene and the cleanliness of her ward, but she was also a wonderful, caring, dedicated nursing sister.

My first impression of Ward B was of Sister McIvor greeting me at the door; an immaculate vision, from the stiff frilly cap perched high on her sandy hair and tied under her chin with a neat bow, to the starched spotless white apron covering her tailored navy dress. Her only ornaments – a well-polished military medal pinned next to her Royal Nursing Corps badge, and a silver embossed ring worn on the third finger of her left hand.

New Year's Eve

Gwen came back from a visit to the dentist in great excitement. She had shared the ambulance with a male patient from Ward A. This adventure in itself was a thrill to Gwen, who often invented a toothache to relieve the boredom of her long residence in the Sanatorium.

She was made for excitement and could conjure it up from the smallest excursion. But this was different, she was bubbling with news and could hardly wait for the ambulance attendant to leave so that she could divulge it to the rest of us. She said that her companion on the dentist visit had told her that the men on Ward A were arranging a party that very night to celebrate New Years' Eve – and most important of all we were invited to attend. It had been well planned, with a couple of male patients who were on afternoon hours organising the beer and refreshments. It needed synchronised timing but it could be done. Night Sister would be in the nurses' home at midnight having her meal, and the ward nurses would be sat in the kitchens having theirs, giving us exactly thirty minutes of freedom in which to climb over the balcony and take a short cut through the shrubbery to Ward A.

There was a buzz of nervous animation as the day went on, and by mid-afternoon Sister McIvor's suspicious mind was working overtime. She had noted that our pulse rates and temperatures were up and instinctively knew that something was afoot. Before going off duty for the day she stood for a while at the door, her steely gaze going from bed to bed, a questioning look in her eyes. We all looked back at her with virtuous smiles on our faces, and Gwen cheekily called out "Goodnight Sister, sleep well." With a shrug and a final skeptical look across the veranda she left the ward.

As soon as the lights were off we sneaked one by one to the bathroom to apply lipstick and rouge, and were all tucked up in bed and feigning sleep by the time Night Sister made her first round. There was a deep sigh of relief as she left the ward after telling the night nurse that she would be back at 1 a.m. We heard her heels clipping the gravel drive as she walked down to the nurses' home. We then lay in silence for at least an hour.

In fact I dozed a little, only to wake as Babs touched my shoulder and whispered, "We are going now." I could see shadowy figures putting on their dressing gowns and some already scrambling over the balcony. I felt scared and didn't want to go, but also I felt afraid to stay on the veranda by myself, so quickly joined the exodus from the ward.

We stumbled through the shrubbery catching sleeves on twisted branches, and once I fell, soiling the knees of my pyjama trousers. It was pitch black, our feet were damp and muddy, and we were all panting with the unaccustomed exertion. At last a beckoning torch waved us onto the veranda of Ward A. One of the male patients was waiting to help us up the unlit steps. Everywhere was in darkness, the only relief being the brightly burning coke stove which was giving the veranda its frightening shadows.

As our eyes grew used to the dimness we could see that the ward was an exact copy of ours with twelve beds side by side, but these were all filled with pyjama clad men who stared at us as if we were from another planet. The only other difference was the strange odour which seemed to extend to the whole of their terrace. Ours always carried an aroma of talcum powder, mixed with the pungent smell of menstrual blood, all enveloped in Angie's strong perfume. But this was a sharp pungent smell of shaving soap and sweaty feet, all mingled with the odour of un-emptied urine bottles, and over laden with what I now realise was a heavy dose of male testosterone.

After formal introductions were made we were handed shandy in beakers which had been somewhat tainted by their previous use as toothbrush mugs. There was a general air of embarrassment, with nowhere to sit other than the occupied beds. Even Angie and Gwen didn't show their usual exuberance. Out of necessity we had to remain silent, and could plainly hear the night nurse's knife and fork as she scraped her dinner plate.

After an awkward silence one of our hosts bravely raised his toothbrush mug and whispered, "Happy New Year, ladies," and we all whispered back, "The same to you." A plate of rich tea biscuits was handed round, and one daring soul started to tell jokes, but in a whisper of course, and no one dare laugh as it was obvious by now that the night nurse was on her pudding. We could hear the swish of her spoon as she lapped up cold custard. Just her cup of tea to have, and then she would be back on duty and looking in on the ward.

The party was a non-starter. We wondered what we were doing there, all of us feeling tired, damp and wet-slippered, and most of us beginning to look unwell. Nan took charge. She briskly thanked Ward A for their hospitality and then ushered us out and through the shrubbery to the safety of our own ward, where we all thankfully scrambled back onto the veranda.

A figure who had been sat in the shadows, unseen in the haste to reach our beds, leant forward into the firelight, and in a soft Edinburgh accent said, "Good evening ladies, I trust you have all had a nice evening stroll."

We all sat bolt upright, shocked and full of guilt. But she simply smiled and walked towards the door, and, always knowing how to make us feel ashamed and fearful, turned and said, "X-Rays for everybody tomorrow, and I guarantee your poor bugs will be dancing jigs after such an escapade!"

And as she left, Gwen, never one to give in easily, called out in a mock Scottish accent, "Happy New Year to you too, Sister McIvor."

Knitting for Angels (Janet's Story)

Janet Robinson loved children. Her many nephews and nieces all adored her. She spoilt them all, giving much of her spare time to knitting jumpers and toys for the younger ones, and inventing new games to play when the older ones visited. Everyone said that she would make a wonderful mother herself, but Janet just smiled, and changed the subject. She would dearly love her own family, and knew that she most likely would have been happily married by now with her own baby on her knee, if fate and a speeding car had not deprived her of Peter.

They had been sweethearts since meeting at school, and had become engaged on her eighteenth birthday, both saving hard for their future home, and planning to marry the following year. It was his keenness to save money that had caused him to be walking home from work that dark wet night, when a motorist had skidded into him, killing him instantly. How Janet wished he'd caught a bus instead of worrying about the few pence he was saving.

She had been devastated by his death, and now in her mid-thirties she had resigned herself to spinsterhood. She reasoned that her life wasn't that bad – she lived with her parents in a comfortable home, and enjoyed her job as a receptionist with Doctor Brown at the village surgery. She had good friends, and went on holiday every year with Margaret, whom she'd known since her first day at infant school. Her main passion was knitting. Most evenings would find her sitting with her parents, listening to the radio, her knitting needles furiously clicking as she followed an intricate pattern, only stopping at 10 o'clock to make cocoa for them all. It was only occasionally, when she couldn't sleep, and lay tossing in her bed until the early hours, that she felt unfulfilled. For what, she didn't know, but she knew it wasn't cocoa and knitting.

She had met Ian at a friend's wedding. He was tall and dark, reserved like herself, but with a warmth about him that made her feel special. They went to the cinema together the following week, and met again the next day for a walk across the fields, stopping to buy a drink at the village pub. Janet enjoyed his company and felt at ease with him, and started to take more care of her appearance, feeling young again when she sat in front of her dressing table trying out a new lipstick, or a different way of doing her hair. Even Doctor Brown remarked about her new look of happiness.

It had been a busy week at the surgery, a mobile x-ray unit parked in the drive, and Janet was taking its visitors names and addresses, and directing them where to wait their turn. On the last day the surgery staff were asked to participate too. Janet, engrossed in her new romance thought no more of it, until a few days later, when a grave looking Doctor Brown asked her to come into his office.

"I'm so sorry Janet," he said, "but you have Tuberculosis."

Her x-ray had been positive, her lungs showing the dark shadow that proved she was tubercular. Doctor Brown explained the options and recovery statistics to her, and advised she should go home and rest until a place in a Sanatorium could be arranged.

She left the surgery in shock. She didn't even feel ill. How could she have this disease? Admittedly she had been feeling tired of late, but surely a few early nights would soon cure that? She felt mortified that everyone she had been in contact with must now have x-rays: her parents, siblings and their children, her friend Margaret, and Ian, even Doctor Brown. She became a patient on Ward B the following week, placed between Ruth and Babs on the veranda.

Janet was a very special person, kind and even tempered, always there for us younger patients, finding time and patience to listen to our worries, and having the wisdom to patch up the petty quarrels that sometimes enlivened our day. In no time at all we were all wearing jumpers and bed socks that had been made for us by this manic knitter. I can never remember Janet without seeing her knitting needles, and hearing their demented clicking as she devoured yet another ball of wool. Anyone allowed hours up would be roped in to stretch out their arms, whilst she wound yet another skein. We all marvelled at her speed and dexterity.

Ian came to see her every Sunday and wrote almost every day. Despite her illness she blossomed in his caring devotion. But Janet's tuberculosis was persistent. A year's bed-rest had made no improvement, and she was not responding to the wonder drug Streptomycin. Her left lung was slowly being eaten away by the disease. After a while Doctor Paul suggested that the only possible cure was to have her lung removed. Janet, desperate to be well, agreed to the operation. This major surgery meant a trip to Warwick Hospital where such procedures were undertaken.

The night before her departure, permission was given for a special visiting hour. Her parents and Ian came, and for the last ten minutes her parents left them alone. After they had left and the screens were removed we could see that she was positively glowing. She held up her left hand to show us the glittering diamond ring she was wearing. Ian had asked her to marry him, and she had accepted. Forgetting bed-rest, we all clambered out of bed and rushed over to kiss and congratulate her.

The next morning she went off to Warwick, a big smile on her face as she waved goodbye to us all. We felt so pleased for her. This operation was going to be her passport out of the Sanatorium, and a chance of a happy life with Ian. Her operation was due to start at 9 a.m. the next morning. After breakfast we were all unusually quiet as we fixed our eyes on the clock, our thoughts with Janet being wheeled to the operating theatre. We knew it was a long operation and we would have no news until later in the day, but our thoughts remained with her.

It was during rest period that Sister McIvor came into the ward and sat by Eileen's bed, and gently whispered in her ear. Eileen immediately burst into tears. The rest of us didn't need a verbal message. We knew by Sister's grave face and Eileen's sobs that Janet was no longer with us. She had died whilst still under the anaesthetic. Her heart had simply given up.

Our sadness was immense. She had been so confident and happy the day before, with so much to look forward to. We were angry that life had been so cruel to her, and also a little afraid for our own futures. This savage disease was totally indiscriminate.

May you always rest in peace, Janet. I like to think that wherever she might be, she is reunited with Peter, and is madly knitting warm jumpers for all the angels around her.

A Cuckoo in the Nest

We still had a vacant bed on the veranda. The third one down that had been empty since Janet's death was a constant reminder of her loss. Its pristine immaculate bedspread and tidy locker gave us a daily twinge of grief at her absence, and a renewed awareness of our own vulnerability.

Usually if there was no new intake due, Sister McIvor would move a patient from the main ward onto the veranda. Often someone she felt might benefit from younger company, or perhaps a disruptive patient whom she wanted to keep an eye on, the office being adjacent to the veranda.

The following Monday, despite it being the morning rest hour, we were all aware that a new patient was due to be admitted. A hot water bottle was placed in the empty bed and Nurse Bumstead screened it off from view. Mid-morning an ambulance came up the drive, stopping at the entrance to Ward B, and Sister McIvor went out to greet it. A few minutes later a bundled-up figure sat in a wheelchair was pushed on to the veranda, and taken behind the screens to be officially admitted.

It was always exciting when a new patient came in. It was mainly an anticipation of some diversion to our lives, and the knowledge that despite her illness this person had until now been free, and breathing the air of freedom that was denied to us. She could tell us of the latest fashion, or the music scene, and perhaps had recently been to the cinema; all the things that our incarceration kept us from.

I recognised the new admission as soon as Nurse Bumstead pulled back the screens, and I was horrified. It was Josie Taylor, a fellow pupil from the High School. My first thought was of bewilderment that she should have Tuberculosis. She was a big hefty girl, the captain of the hockey team, and never known to have an illness in her life. She was also a bully, and had made my life at school utterly wretched.

She was a clever bully, always managing to fool teachers and friends into believing that she was a caring person: the first one a teacher would pick to be a monitor, or to be a mentor to a new girl. The daughter of a vicar, she radiated her Christianity as a front, covering up the nasty, malicious person she really was. She had succeeded in making my life miserable, and was probably partly responsible for my dislike of school. Her favourite trick was to walk to the bus stop with me pretending friendship, and then she would snatch my bus fare away, leaving me to walk home alone. If I took a Mars Bar to school for a playtime snack, it would be sure to find its way into Josie's pocket. She would demand a bite from my lunchtime apple, knowing full well that afterwards I would give her the whole one, not wanting to eat it after she had taken a bite. She mocked my lack of skill at games, and would slyly hit my ankles with her hockey stick, always profusely apologising when the teacher noticed my limp.

And now she was here, sitting up in the bed that had belonged to nice gentle Janet, who would never have said a hurtful word to anyone – I felt quite devastated, and unlike the rest of the ward I burrowed down under the sheets, not wanting to acknowledge our acquaintance. As usual with a new admittance everyone was firing questions at her, anxious to have news of the outside world. She was as devious as ever, playing the part of 'poor little me' to perfection.

In no time at all she was bosom friends with everyone, giggling with Gwen, and holding court around her bed each night. She was deferential to the staff, promising Sister McIvor that she would never do anything wrong to jeopardize her recovery, and then jumping out of bed as soon as Sister McIvor went off duty, despite being on strict bed rest. There was no communication between us; she acted as if I was a complete stranger, and I was happy to comply.

It didn't take very long for her poisonous true nature to come to the fore. I soon realised after Sunday's visitors had gone that she was doing a lot of whispered gossiping, whilst looking directly at me. It was quite obvious that she was back to her old tricks, and her new cronies were being taken in as much as fellow pupils had been.

Soon her venom reached me. Whilst cleaning our teeth in the bathroom that evening, Ruth remarked how sad it was that Josie's elderly father was not able to visit her, as the steep hill was too much for him, and how wicked it was that those who had a car refused to give him a lift. I immediately knew what the whispering was about; my father was the only visitor with a car, and in fact Josie's home was not far from mine.

But what she didn't tell them was that her father, despite his vicar's garb, was just as nasty as she was. My parents couldn't forget his quick dismissal of my application to join the Brownies, or earlier banning me from Sunday school, and his refusal to conduct my sister's wedding – all based on the fact that our family did not attend his church. And he had not endeared himself to my father when he ordered a new bedroom suite; not just any bedroom suite, but the most expensive one in our shop, and whilst waiting for its delivery came back to add a deluxe mattress to the order. And later, when asked to pay the bill he suggested to my father that seeing the furniture was for the vicarage he presumed it would be deemed a gift to the church. I was at school and missed out on my father's colourful reply, but later that evening I was sitting in the delivery van when he forcibly fetched the goods back.

So there was little cordiality between our families, and despite it not being the Christian thing to do, I could understand why no lift was offered. But of course, this didn't help the muttering and discord that Josie had brought to the veranda.

Sister McIvor was quick to notice my discomfort when she had kindly asked if I would like Josie's bed pushed next to mine. Having seen I was a little depressed, she thought it might cheer me up to have a young person alongside me. She was taken back by my instant look of horror, and emphatic reply. The very thought of exchanging the quiet, sweet natured Amy for nasty Josie, was enough to send me into a flood of tears. Sister McIvor looked puzzled by my obvious distress, and reassured me that if I was so against it she would leave things as they were. That night my temperature and pulse rate were unusually high, and I was given a sleeping tablet and kept an eye on by night sister.

Things didn't improve, and I was mortified the following week when my parents arrived punctually, and her father came an hour late, puffing and wheezing from his walk up the hill. The whispered persecution started again. I felt helpless because I knew my father wouldn't relent, having no time for vicars, and especially this particular one, and would have probably driven past if he had seen him collapsed on the pavement.

Things started to get nasty when she told everyone that the reason my family didn't go to church was because my father was a Jew. Her reliance on this statement was fuelled by the fact that amongst other businesses he ran he was also a licensed moneylender. This led her on to more vindictive remarks, usually muttered as I passed her bed on my way to the bathroom. "No wonder your nose is so big," was a favourite, and warning people to clean out the bath well if I had been using it.

She was clever, her remarks were made only in the company of her new followers, and even they had the grace to look ashamed. The verbal bullying was having an effect on my recovery. I had lost my appetite, and most of the confidence that six months on the veranda had given me. I was unsure whom I could trust, feeling that nobody would believe me, and yet knowing that most of the patients were exactly the same people they had been before Josie's arrival.

But she continued to play the role of a sweet kind girl, who if she could, would help anyone. She was taken off bed rest after the first month and this made things worse as she was free to follow me to the bathroom and use even more abuse. I began to ignore my need for the toilet, waiting until someone else went in, and then scurrying after them to avoid being alone with Josie.

Fortunately I had a saviour. Angie was nobody's fool, and had in her youth fought off both verbal and physical abuse. She had observed my reluctance to be alone with Josie, and as she told me later, had seen through the little madam from the start. Her kindness broke the barrier I had started to put up, and I told her the whole sorry tale. She held my hand and dried the tears that were now freely falling. When I'd finished telling her, I felt so much better for sharing the load I had been carrying by myself.

Typically Angie, she was all for storming across the veranda to challenge Josie. "I will sort the little madam out," she said.

I begged her not to, and said I was going to leave as soon as I got my hours up, and was able to get dressed. "I'm going to run away," I told her.

The very next morning, as soon as Sister McIvor came on duty she went straight to Josie's bed, dropped the wheels and without a word said, pushed her off the veranda, across the hall, and into the main ward, with Nurse Bumstead close behind pulling the locker. Everyone stared open mouthed; no one had ever been taken off the veranda in such a way before. A few minutes later a new patient's bed was put in its place. Sister McIvor had done a swap, and we had certainly got the best of it. Anne, the newcomer, was lovely; a warm hearted middle aged woman who almost immediately fitted in.

I'd not seen Angie go into Sister McIvor's office after our talk, but as Josie's bed was being removed she gave me a wink and a knowing nod of her head. Later Gwen and Ruth came to me and apologised for any hurt that they might have caused, and said they were glad that Josie had been moved, as the whole veranda had felt the discord that she'd provoked. We hugged. My whole world seemed lighter, and I decided to stay.

Goodbye Momma (Rebecca's Story)

When I entered the Sanatorium, Rebecca Levy had been a staff nurse on Ward B for a couple of years. She was a calm soft spoken person, with an efficient manner that made you feel immediately at ease. Her movements were always very precise, and although she didn't have the easy relationship with her patients that Nurse Bumstead had, she was respected for her competent nursing skills.

Despite speaking excellent English she had a slight guttural accent that betrayed her German birth. But she didn't look like the accepted stereotype of a Nordic Fraulein; her hair was dark, and her deep set brown eyes were sombre with a permanent look of tragedy – and her story was a tragic one.

She was born in Hamburg in 1928, the only child of a wealthy Jewish couple whose ancestors had lived in Germany for generations. Her father and two uncles had fought with distinction in the German army during the First World War, and had always considered themselves true compatriots, their allegiance firstly to the country of their birth, their Jewish birth right coming secondary.

Her father, Joseph Levy, was a director of the family business, which consisted of a large department store in Hamburg's main shopping area. They lived in a comfortable apartment in a tree lined avenue situated in an affluent part of the city. Rebecca went to a small private school, and lived a privileged and happy life. In the school holidays, she and her mother Hester would take a tram to the city centre and visit her father in his office on the top floor of the department store. He would proudly take her by the hand and using the recently installed lift, they would descend to the basement where a tearoom was situated. Rebecca loved this treat, being made much of by the staff, and usually having delicious cakes to eat and a hot creamy chocolate drink. After her father had returned to his office, she and her mother would visit each department, trying on shoes and fashionable clothes. And whilst Rebecca played shops with a young assistant, her mother would have her hair waved in the salon on the second floor.

Although not orthodox, they kept the Jewish Sabbath, and celebrated the religious days with large family gatherings at Rebecca's maternal grandparents' home. She had many aunts, uncles and cousins on both sides of her family. Sometimes at these family gatherings there would be serious discussions about Germany's future, and the possibility of an approaching war. There was some concern about the current wave of anti-Semitism that was increasing across the country. The government seemed to be encouraging it, and many German Jews were expelled from work in any professional capacity, and there was talk of Jews not being allowed into further education, or theatres and cinemas. Rebecca's family thought it was being exaggerated by scaremongers, and were confident that as long standing German Citizens they would not be affected.

Things got more serious towards the end of the decade. Hamburg's extensive Jewish commerce and manufacturing businesses were being requisitioned and taken over by non-Jewish Germans. Within months, Joseph Levy had lost his department store, and Rebecca was expelled from her school. Jews all over Germany were beginning to realise that they were not invincible to this madness that was sweeping the country.

Many were desperately trying to leave, but visas were expensive and difficult to obtain. Rebecca's mother had a brother in America who invited them to come and live with him. They queued for days trying to get an exit visit, but to no avail, and when neighbours started to disappear in the night to unknown destinations, Joseph was worried about the safety of his precious daughter. He had heard about a scheme to get children out of danger by taking them to England. He contacted an old business friend in Berlin who was helping to organise the transport. His only thought was to get Rebecca out of the danger that he now recognised was very real. Rebecca's mother was loath to part with her and strongly opposed the plan. But as the restrictions on Jewish life increased and more of their friends and family disappeared, she came to realise that she had to put her daughter's safety first, and agreed to allow Joseph to try and get a place for the child on one of the so called 'kinder transports'.

With great difficulty and with much bribing, he managed to get Rebecca a seat on a train leaving that weekend. He was not to know it at the time, but it was the very last kinder train to leave Germany as the Second World War started within days of its departure.

Rebecca Levy was just ten years of age when she waved her parents goodbye on the platform, before boarding the train that was to take her to safety in England. In one hand she clutched a small suitcase which was all she was allowed to take, and in the other a precious doll which was a farewell present from her parents. Before kissing her goodbye, her father told her that hidden inside its hollow china head was gold jewellery which he was entrusting to her to keep safe until he and her mother could get visas to join her in England.

The final goodbye was hard. Rebecca was confused and unhappy to be thrust on a train with strangers, and sad to see her distraught mother weeping in her father's arms. The guard waved his flag. A whistle blew and Rebecca rushed to an open window and called out "Goodbye, Momma" as she waved one last time to the by now receding figures still standing stiffly on the station platform. She was never to see either of them again.

Rebecca's memories of that journey were vague, although she could still recall the moment of panic as they crossed the German frontier, when a border guard pulled the doll from her hand, but returned it when she offered her gold watch in its place. The whole train load of passengers had breathed a great sigh of relief when they had at last been allowed to cross the border into Holland, where they were fed a hot meal by kindly Dutch women, before continuing their journey to England.

It had been a bewildering arrival. The children and the few adults who had accompanied them were taken into a large dockside shed where the Red Cross gave them mugs of tea and a packet of sandwiches each. But to the children's dismay they couldn't eat them despite their hunger. The unwitting helpers had used pork luncheon meat as a filling.

Some of the children were met by English relatives who gave them tearful hugs and kisses, before leading them away to new homes in Jewish communities all over the country. Others like Rebecca stood forlorn and frightened, not knowing where they were going. Eventually some coaches arrived for them, and the children were driven off to a town further up the coast. It was dark when they arrived and they were quickly put to bed in what seemed to be wooden huts. Rebecca, feeling cold, tired and hungry, tightly hugged her doll to her chest and cried herself to sleep.

The next morning she realised she was billeted in a holiday camp, which had been commandeered to house the refugee children. No longer tired and having had a substantial breakfast, her natural curiosity took over from the heartbreak of the night before, and with some other girls she set off to explore the camp. Later she was given a stamped postcard to send to her parents to tell of her safe arrival.

Sadly, this failed to arrive as hostilities between Germany and England were about to begin.

Rebecca spent the war years living in Derbyshire. She had been offered a home by a country doctor and his wife. It had taken a long time for her to adapt to a totally alien lifestyle, but with the kindness and patience of her foster carers she slowly adjusted to her new life. She missed her parents and family very much, but as time passed her recollections dimmed, as did her German. She started to think in English and to even dream in her new language. Sometimes as she looked at the china doll and the fading photographs of her mother and father she found herself straining to remember that other life. Her Jewish heritage seemed just a distant dream. She visited the local church with the doctor and his wife, joined the village tennis club and made new friends.

She had given up expecting letters, although it was hard each birthday to have no greetings from her family. The doctor had promised that as soon as the war ended he would help her to make contact with her relatives again. And when at last Germany surrendered and peace was celebrated, her only thought was to be reunited with her beloved parents. She wrote to their old address in Hamburg and anxiously awaited a reply. And when she had no response, the doctor contacted the Red Cross to ask for help in tracing their whereabouts.

He explained to Rebecca that Germany was in such post-war turmoil that it could take a long time to reunite families. Privately, he was worried that her family could have perished in the mass slaughter of Jews that Germany had instigated. He tried to shield Rebecca from the horror stories that were featured in the papers and newsreels, but she was aware that many Jews had died in concentration camps, and prayed that her parents had survived.

The day before her 17th birthday she received the confirmation that she had dreaded. Joseph and Hester Levy, along with all their relations, had been murdered in the gas chambers of the notorious Belsen camp. She had lost everybody.

Five years later she took the position of staff nurse in the Sanatorium. She had done her general training and wanted to gain experience in tubercular nursing before emigrating to Israel. She had heard there was a great need for such skills to work with the mass influx of Jewish refugees that were pouring into the new country from every corner of the earth. Despite her affection for the doctor and his wife, she felt the need to live amongst her own people again.

Staff nurse Levy moved to live and work in Tel Aviv twelve months later.

Visitors

The most important dates on the ward calendar, which were always ringed in red crayon, were the monthly visits of Dr Paul, such was his power over our lives. We existed from one month to the next, always with the expectation that some miracle would occur and the sick would get well, and our long-awaited freedom would be granted.

The weeks between his visits were just intervals that we endured, a time in which we sustained ourselves by the hope that the next month would be the one that gave us back our lives. The other red ringed dates were the weekly visiting hours – every Sunday afternoon, 2 p.m. until 3.30 p.m. This was anticipated the whole week, our thoughts and preparations beginning each Sunday evening within hours of that day's visitors leaving.

The time in between would pass, our routine was such that the days merged with each other. Meals, medication and rest periods gave a structure to our lives, and the loving companionship we shared allowed a feeling of unity.

The veranda fostered a unique comradeship. Twelve women of different generations and diverse backgrounds living in such close proximity made for an intimacy of fierce protectiveness, and an instinctive awareness of each other's fears. We were as much a family as the relatives who visited us, and it was often hard for them to understand our solidarity.

The excitement would be intense by Sunday dinnertime, a shame, as it was the best dinner of the week and quite often we were too agitated to enjoy it. On visiting days, we would have an early meal followed by a short rest period, but nobody rested. The time would be spent checking make-up and hairdos in the small hand mirrors that we all kept in our lockers.

At approximately five minutes to two, Sister McIvor would walk the length of the veranda, straightening the odd counterpane, flicking imaginary dust off a bedside locker, and all the while fixing us with a steely glance that without her uttering a word warned us to behave and not disturb our bugs. She would then stand at the ward's main door, checking her watch, counting the seconds until it was exactly 2 p.m., and only then would she open the doors, graciously greeting the visitors who had been patiently standing outside, some for an hour or more.

We all knew who would be first on the veranda, and would nod to each other as Eva's husband, Robert, strode down the ward, a beaming smile on his face and his eyes fixed intently on his wife. A shy man, he was embarrassed by our scrutiny, but he would have faced worse just to sit by her side and hold her hand.

A noisy clamour at the door usually announced Gwen's sisters, a melee of buxom, beautiful girls arguing with Sister McIvor about her strict rule of only two visitors to a bed. But once she had returned to her office they all crept in anyway, and I think she was well aware of this, but had to be seen to show her authority.

Being preoccupied with our own visitors didn't deter our watchfulness of others. In the early days we could see Eileen's distress at the absence of her fiancé Johnny, and I'm sure that, if he had ever shown his face after the dismissive letter he sent her, we would have all risen from our beds and attacked him.

Ruth would sit placidly knitting, undeterred by her lack of visitors, knowing that one day her postman would come. However, she was never alone for long as Gwen's visitors would soon overlap around her bed too. Nan's mother would always come. She helped Nan out of bed and supported her as she stood on a chair in the bathroom to wave to her children, who, accompanied by an aunt, had climbed the hill at the back of the Sanatorium to enable them to catch a glimpse of their mother.

Elsa's husband never missed a second of their Sunday's visit. Her Joe would be just a few steps behind Eva's Robert. In fact, the two men had struck up a friendship and usually went for a drink together on the way home.

Babs' parents would sometimes arrive late, having further to come, and it was a steep hill for her mother to push the wheelchair up. They would be laden with gifts for her, often things they could ill afford.

Angie had few visitors. Occasionally one of her barmaid friends would pop in for a while, but usually she would put on her dressing gown and give herself an unofficial hour up by sitting with Amy, who after Derek went abroad never had anyone come either.

Angie would laugh and say, "Nobody wants to know us, my duck."

Dottie had regular visitors from the Queens Hotel. All her old workmates came to see her, and kept her well informed of various guests' antics. There was always loud laughter from her bedside.

Janet also had plenty of visitors, and was quite overwhelmed when her previous boss, Dr Brown, called in to see her. And of course, Ian was always by her side, staying on for a few extra minutes after her mother left. He was a lovely man and we were all very happy when they got engaged.

My parents came every week, my father striding down the veranda in his best navy serge, and his gold watch and chain across his waistcoat. He was at first taken for my grandfather, being twenty years older than my mother. She would be a few feet behind him, hampered by the bags of books I had requested, the small bookcase at the end of the veranda being very limited. Having been a constant user of both the public library and Boots' private one, I always had a ready list of my favourite authors, and when that was completed an obliging librarian would select an assortment for my mother to bring. I was reading on average one a day, sometimes two. Once read, the parcel of books would have to go to the de-contamination shed at the side of the porters' lodge to be fumigated before my mother could take them back to the library. This caring librarian set me off on a very diverse reading adventure, which saw me plough my way through the classics, giving me a lifelong love of Jane Austen, and the works of Dickens. On reflection, I realise that the librarian had no idea of my age as some of the reading was definitely adult.

My parents obviously felt uncomfortable with their surroundings, my father having little to say, and on occasion having a little doze, but it was enough that he was there and holding my hands tightly in his strong ones. My mother would gossip and take an interest in the other patients, often talking more to their visitors than to me.

The only time I wished I'd had no visitors was the Sunday afternoon she brought along a neighbour of ours. My father was busy with his haymaking, and so Mrs White, a woman I detested, came in his place. She was small and plump, with beady little eyes that seemed to see right through you, and a vicious tongue from which few were spared. I was upset that she had come and the visit was not a success; in fact, my mother realised my anger and departed early.

It was many years before I found out the true reason for her coming. My parents, feeling vaguely ashamed at my contracting Tuberculosis and being incarcerated in a Sanatorium, had kept it very quiet, just saying I was away for a few months. This was enough for Mrs White's fertile mind, and soon a rumour was being spread that I had gone away to have a baby. This was ridiculous. Until then I had been ill and not left the house for almost a year, and had never had contact or conversation with a boy in my life. When I found out, I was furious with my mother for giving credit to her scandalous gossip, and for bringing Mrs White to the hospital to prove it a lie. My father was angry at the time too, saying she should have been told to go to hell.

Sister McIvor would come out of her office at exactly 3.30 p.m. and stand at the ward's entrance ringing the large brass bell. These strident peals would echo down the row of beds, and the visitors would hurriedly gather up our bundles of washing and say hasty goodbyes, in some cases with great relief, having run out of conversation a while back. Some would linger, bravely risking Sister McIvor's sharp tongue for the sake of one more hug or kiss. And the first two through the door were usually the last to leave.

Nobody had much appetite for the early tea which was served as soon as the final visitor had departed, but this was not surprising as most of us had a locker full of home baked treats. With the aftermath of the day's excitement, the veranda would fall silent, most of us, if truthful, quite exhausted by the feverish pitch we had reached in anticipation of another Sunday.

However, by suppertime, conversation had already reached the point where discussion was in full flow about who would swap a blouse or sweater for next week's visit.

Although visiting day was so eagerly awaited it was also something of a damp squib. Once the visitors had gone we returned to the reality of where we were, with the knowledge that they had gone back into a world that we were no longer a part of.

A Hard Life (Amy's Story)

Amy's stay on Ward B was short. Her Tuberculosis was in its last stage when she was carried onto the veranda, her young body painfully thin. A racking cough shook her slight frame, and left her breathless. She had a beautiful angelic face, with a deceptive look of innocence. But her language was colourful, learnt in the slums as a child, and used as a protective shield in her teens. Between distressing spasms of coughing she would talk freely about her life. She had no bitterness or anger, just a quiet acceptance of her fate.

At nine years of age, Amy had been the eldest of the four Williams children. Her brother Alan was only three and her twin sisters still in nappies. The long gap between Amy and the other three had been due to her father's war service. Maggie, her mother, had been overjoyed at his safe return, and Alan, the result of her elation, was born nine months later. The twins, she always said, had been a little mistake.

Amy could still remember the good times when they had all been happy. Sadly, the little ones had only known the poverty and deprivation that followed. But she remembered the cosy miner's cottage that they had lived in, and the good standard of living that her father's wages provided.

She could also vividly recall the sound of the pit siren, followed by the pounding of many feet, and the shouts of their neighbours as they raced to the pit head. Her mother had left her with the little ones whilst she too ran to join them. There had been a bad fall at the pit face – six men were trapped, including her father. She would also never forget the hushed silence when his dead body was carried into their front room, and then the sound of her mother's screaming shattering the quiet.

The bereaved family had a week's notice to leave the colliery-owned property. Her mother was distraught, still inconsolable with grief. The young widow had no close relatives to turn to, and her in-laws, always disliking her, had offered no help. She took the children and their possessions and moved to the nearby town, renting two rooms in the basement of a large crumbling Victorian villa. The basement had no running water or electricity – the family relied on an ancient outside pump for their water supply, candles for light, and an old rusty range for heating and cooking. A broken lavatory at the bottom of the overgrown garden, and the cracked stone sink in a leaking outhouse, were their only sanitary facilities.

Maggie took her widowhood and changed circumstances badly. She missed her husband and the comforts of her lost home, and despaired of managing financially on the small widow's pension which was all she had. Taking Amy out of school to care for the little ones, she took a job at a nearby laundry. The work was hard but paid enough to feed and clothe them all. At the end of a day spent in the hot sweaty ironing rooms, Maggie would feel reluctant to return to the stuffy basement. She would linger awhile in the cosy snug bar of the 'Red Lion', where she could forget for a while her sadness. She started to extend her visits, sometimes staying until closing time, not wanting to face the reality of four hungry children waiting for her in the dingy rooms that she refused to call home.

Amy, waiting anxiously for her return, would put the babies in the old worn out pram and taking Alan by the hand, go out in search of her. Maggie would grudgingly leave the warmth and brightness of the pub and follow them home, calling at the corner shop to buy a loaf of bread and a pot of jam for their tea. Sometimes, if the company in the snug was generous and convivial, she would briefly excuse herself to answer Amy's call, and take out crisps and lemonade to the waiting hungry children.

Maggie started to drink more frequently at the 'Red Lion', also buying spirits at the off licence to take back to the basement – to help her through the night. Soon she was finding it difficult to get up and go to work. After a few absences, the manager dismissed her. The meagre pension she received hardly kept her in alcohol, or paid the rent, and the children suffered even more. Whilst Maggie slept off her drunken binges, Amy would search her clothes or handbag, taking any small change she could find to buy milk and bread for the little ones.

It was a wonderful treat when a kindly man who had been lucky on the horses tossed her half-a-crown. "Get yourself some fish and chips, love," he said. Saving a shilling for emergencies, she bought chips for them all, leaving her mother's portion on the table when she went to bed. Next morning, they were still there, and Maggie was lying on the floor, fully dressed and loudly snoring, her left eye bruised and already turning black – yet another fight after the pub had closed. Amy covered her over with an old coat and left her to sleep it off.

Gradually their few possessions started to disappear, one day a chair, the next some bed linen, and one morning the old pram had gone.

Maggie had to get her drinking money and nothing was sacred. Soon there was very little left in the two rooms of any value. Everything had been sold or pawned to buy alcohol. Some nights their mother didn't come home at all. Amy, shivering with the little ones on their only remaining mattress, would stay awake until the pub had closed, listening hopefully for Maggie's stumbling steps. Many nights she listened in vain, her mother going home with anyone who would buy her that extra drink.

Despite the poverty of the area, Amy and her siblings stood out as exceptionally needy, poorly clothed, pale and underweight. People felt sorry for them. Their mother's drinking and bawdy behaviour had made her notorious, but nobody told the authorities of the children's neglect; it wasn't the sort of district where you informed on a neighbour.

Early one morning Amy heard Maggie struggling to open the basement door. Running across the room, she was just in time to catch her trembling mother before she collapsed on to the stone floor. Half dragging the semi-conscious figure, she managed to get her onto the old mattress where she lay sweating and moaning. The other children, now fully awake, looked at their mother with fear. She was thrashing about in agony and calling out for help.

Amy, in panic, ran out into the street, but at that early hour it was deserted. She ran to the 'Red Lion', shouting and banging on the door until the landlord came down to see what all the fuss was about.

"Please help my mother," she begged. "She's really very ill."

"Very drunk, more like," he said. But he followed her back to the basement, seeing at first glance that Maggie, writhing in pain on the mattress, was indeed seriously ill.

An ambulance was called and she was rushed to the emergency room at the local hospital. She had a burst appendix, and her body, weakened by alcohol abuse, was too feeble to fight the peritonitis that was already poisoning her.

Amy clung to her mother as she was put into the ambulance, and Maggie, lucid for a few seconds, gripped her hand and said, "I'm so sorry Amy, so very sorry. Make sure the little ones are looked after." She smiled through her pain, and for a brief moment looked like the loving mother she used to be.

These were her last words. She died during the night, delirious and alone.

Later that morning Amy opened the door to two smartly dressed ladies. The elder of the two shook her hand and said, "We have come to take you all to 'Rosemount Lodge' until Mummy's better."

The lodge was a large children's home situated on the other side of town. Alan and the twins were moved on the next day to a smaller home which housed babies and younger children, and Amy was taken to a temporary foster home.

She was broken-hearted at being parted from the little ones. They had looked bewildered when placed in the care workers' car, and their screams stayed with her for a long time afterwards, along with the pinched, frightened face of Alan, who stared bleakly back at her from the rear window.

By the time Amy was informed of her mother's death, Maggie had already been laid to rest in a pauper's grave. Amy cried bitter tears, not for the mother who had neglected them all, but for the pretty and happy one of her earlier memories, the one they had lost a long time ago.

The temporary foster home became permanent, but Amy was not settled there. She fretted for the little ones, having had no contact with them since they were taken away. Once she missed school and spent the whole day searching without success for the home they were living in. Another time she ran away, heading back to the empty basement, forcing open the door and sleeping rough on the floor, but the police soon found her and she was returned to the foster home.

Mrs Brenner, her foster mother was kind, but very strict. Having two grown-up daughters of her own, she was of the opinion that girls of Amy's age needed a lot of careful watching. Mr Brenner was an insurance agent and worked most evenings, only staying in on Saturday nights whilst his wife went to the pictures with her sister. He was left to supervise the three foster children's bed times. Amy felt uncomfortable when he stood too close to her as she cleaned her teeth. His breath reeked of alcohol, reminding her of her mother's drinking.

Over the next three years she occasionally saw her brother and sisters. Visits would be arranged for birthdays and at Christmas. She would excitedly wait for these reunions, saving her meagre pocket money for weeks ahead to buy them all small gifts and sweets. The twins were no longer the babies she had cared for. She was cheered to see their plump bodies and rosy cheeks, but was saddened to see the lack of recognition in their eyes when she ran to greet them – they clung to their carers' hands, shyly reaching out to take the sweets from the sister who was now a stranger. Her brother seemed happy and content, chatting endlessly about the football team he was in, and the seaside holiday he was soon to go on. After these visits Amy always felt sad and depressed, and would cry herself to sleep.

She was growing to be a very pretty girl. At fifteen she had a nice figure, shiny blonde hair, and a sweet, shy smile. Mr Brenner still made her feel uneasy. Not liking the sly glances he gave her when no one else was looking, and the way he brushed against her in passing, she always avoided being alone with him. When her foster mother had to go into hospital for a minor operation it was decided that Amy and the other foster children were old enough to manage on their own during the day, knowing they would have Mr Brenner's supervision at bedtime.

He made his move the second night after the girls had gone to bed. He followed Amy upstairs shortly after she had said goodnight. She had felt no fear, thinking he was going to use the bathroom, but he came into her room instead. He smiled at her, and leaning across the bed clumsily tried to kiss her, the stink of his beery breath making her retch. She tried to push him away as he started to fumble with her pyjama top, but this only increased his ardour.

In panic she reached out, and grabbing the bedside lamp brought it smashing down on to his head. She felt his body stiffen and then relax. She pushed him away and rolled out of bed. Mr Brenner lay face down on her pillow, a gaping open wound on the back of his head, the pillowcase staining red beneath him. Paralysed with fear, Amy stared at him, believing he was dead, and then the thought that he might come alive again jolted her into action. Shocked and trembling, she quickly dressed, and throwing a few clothes into her bag, she took the little money she had and fled.

That first night she walked the empty streets until daybreak, buying coffee and toast at an early morning cafe, where she sat too tired and despondent to ponder her immediate future. She knew she could never return to her foster home, and it was possible that Mr Brenner was dead. In that case the police would be already looking for her. Whilst sipping her hot coffee and mentally discarding all the foolish plans that came to mind, she became aware of the cafe filling up with a noisy chattering crowd.

Two swarthy faced women with gold rings flashing in their ears approached her table, carrying hot bacon sandwiches and mugs of tea. Amy realised that they were travelling people from the fair which had been in the market square over the Easter holidays, and now it was all packed up ready to move on. On a sudden impulse, she asked if they needed any extra help. The women eyed her with suspicion at first, asking where her mum and dad were, and why was she on her own at this early hour. Amy decided to tell them the truth, only omitting the fact that she had left Mr Brenner for dead.

The two women conferred with the owner of the fair, a tall rugged man who glanced over at Amy with a doubtful expression on his face. But the women who felt sorry for the obviously distressed girl were persuasive, and he came across to Amy's table, looked intently in her face, and seemed to make up his mind about her. Walking away, he turned to the older woman and said, "She can share your van."

As the sky lightened, the convoy of lorries and caravans left the town. Amy, who was perched high between the woman and the driver in the leading truck, didn't look back.

She stayed with the fair for the next three years, travelling the length and breadth of the country, getting used to never stopping in one place for long, always managing to send a birthday card to her brother and sisters from wherever she was at the time. With the constant moving and no permanent address, she felt safe to keep contact in this way.

After a while she began to think she had never known any other life. The work was hard as the women had warned her, but the travellers treated her well, the owner always keeping a protective eye on her. Every Easter the fair returned to Amy's home town. She always remained inside the van, not wanting anyone to recognise her. She longed to see her brother and sisters, but was too afraid of the consequences.

One Easter, when peering through the van window, she was shocked to see Mr and Mrs Brenner strolling arm in arm across the fairground. So he hadn't died. Having thought of him as dead for so long, it was strange to see him alive and well. She felt almost sorry that he had survived, but at least she wasn't a fugitive any more, though she still stayed hidden inside the van, unwilling to meet him face to face.

The following winter was a bitterly cold one, the toughest season for the travelling workers. Cruel biting winds would blow across the fairground, the travellers shivering behind their stalls, stamping their freezing feet and cupping icy hands to blow some warmth in them. Dismantling their equipment in the early hours, they were often soaked to the skin by driving rain, or slipping and sliding on frost bound fields, racing against time to erect the fair once more.

Amy's health suffered. Never robust, and disadvantaged by her earlier hardships, she struggled to survive the harsh winters on the road. She became too ill to work, and lay in the van sweating or shivering, whichever her erratic temperature dictated. She coughed until her small frame could take no more, and refused any food that the concerned travellers prepared for her.

When in the early hours of the morning she became delirious, the worried fair owner drove her to the Out Patients department of the nearest hospital. Carrying her from his truck wrapped in a warm blanket he laid her gently at the door, and after ringing the bell drove away, eager to catch up with his travelling companions who were already well on their way to their next destination.

Her journey was still not complete – she joined us on the veranda a few days later. We all realised how ill she was when she was placed in the bed next to Sister McIvor's office, the space that was always reserved for the very sick. Despite her fragility she was always eager to talk, and after the lights were switched off she would whisper stories of her life and travels, stopping frequently to take deep shuddering breaths and cough up more sputum.

Her brother Alan was traced and brought to visit her. We could hear them both weeping behind the screens that Sister McIvor had discreetly placed around the bed. The twins, now adopted and happily settled with a new family, were considered too young to visit. Children were not normally allowed into the ward, but Amy had so much wanted to see her brother that an exception was made.

He had brought photographs of them all, and some drawings that her sisters had done at school especially for her, although it was unlikely that they remembered her. It was an emotional scene when he left. The parting was hard for both of them. She cried as if her heart was breaking when he was driven away.

She kept the photographs on her locker where she could see them when first waking, and always kissed each one before the lights were dimmed at night.

We all knew the end was near when she was moved into the small room that had a connecting door to Sister McIvor's office. Doctor Paul had visited her twice that day, and we had heard her shallow breathing, which seemed overloud in the respectful silence of the ward. She slipped quietly and peacefully away in the early hours, none of us sleeping, all thinking our own thoughts of the sadness of her short life.

May you rest in peace, Amy.

The Redhead

A ward full of women was always going to be a hotbed of gossip, and a venue for over-active hormones, the veranda being no exception. Within our restricted world the slightest hint of scandal would quickly spread from bed to bed, often increasing in slander as it travelled. It only took a passing reference to Dr Paul's new bride, which accidentally slipped from Nurse Bumstead's lips whilst changing the sheets on Gwen's bed, to have the ward agog with interest and excitement.

It was common knowledge that Dr Paul was a widower, his wife dying tragically in a swimming accident a few years back. Only Gwen, who had been a patient at the time could remember it happening, and often talked of his anguished appearance when he returned to work after a period of mourning.

He had seemed to be totally engrossed in his duties as the Sanatorium's chief medical officer, with no private life so far as his patients knew, although he had recently been on a skiing trip. The only reason we knew this was because of the previous ward round he'd made, when he was leaning heavily on a walking stick. Eileen overheard him tell Sister McIvor that it was the result of a sprained ankle he'd received whilst on holiday in Switzerland.

It was common knowledge that Gwen was madly in love with him. Her rampant hormones had to have some outlet, and he being saviour and a God-like figure to us all, was the obvious choice of her passionate adoration. She talked about him incessantly, and the high spots of her life were his monthly rounds. I think she always knew he was out of her reach, but was content to worship him from afar, and no one could take her dreams of him away.

She was devastated by Nurse Bumstead's casual words, and went into an unusual depressed silence for the remainder of the day. But her natural exuberance soon came back, and she was prepared to forgive him for the error he had made in marrying someone else.

We were to meet the new bride sooner than expected. She accompanied Dr Paul to the Sanatorium's Christmas lunch. By tradition it was always held a few days before the festivities, allowing patients well enough to go home over Christmas the chance to share it with their fellow patients. Dr Paul always donned an apron and carved the turkey, and Sister McIvor hovered by his side, pouring rich gravy over the sliced poultry before handing the plates to Staff Nurse Levy, to fill with roast potatoes and assorted vegetables, and she would then pass them on to Nurse Bumstead to take to the patients; everybody having their place in the seasonal ritual.

But this year everything was thrown into chaos by the appearance of Dr Paul's new bride. She was young and very beautiful, with long thick red hair that gleamed under the Christmas lights, her strong French accent only adding to her charm. We all glanced from this vision of perfection to Gwen, expecting some explosive reaction. In fact she behaved well, probably as equally stunned as the rest of us, including Sister McIvor, who stood open mouthed as the new Mrs Paul, looking smart in a pretty, frilled apron took over the pouring of the gravy.

The excited gossip afterwards continued well into the New Year, giving us an inexhaustible topic, which Gwen refrained from joining in, only loudly sniffing when the new bride's stunning looks and red hair were remarked on. But she had obviously been thinking hard and quietly making plans.

The Sunday before Dr Paul's next round was due. One of Gwen's sisters handed her a package and had a whispered discussion as to its use. And as soon as the visitors had gone Gwen triumphantly held up a sachet of hair dye. "I'm going to go red," she said. A few of the older patients were dubious, warning her that she already bleached her hair, and the dye might not take. Typically, she shrugged off the warnings and ordered me into the bathroom with her to help make the transformation.

It wasn't quite the result she'd hoped for. As I rubbed the foaming dye into her scalp, her hair slowly turned into a mouldy looking green. I was too scared to tell her, and simply rinsed the dye away, passing her a towel to wrap round her wet locks, and then bolted back into the ward, shaking with what I knew were the inevitable results.

And sure enough, within minutes there was a loud scream from within the bathroom and the door burst open with an hysterical Gwen, yelling that I had turned her hair green and she was going to kill me. Nan, the usual pacifier, took my part, telling her it was the dye's fault, not the shampooer's. And on rescuing the empty sachet it quite clearly stated that it was not to be used on bleached hair.

She did look funny, and we all tried to hide our suppressed laughter as she sat up in bed with a towel wrapped tightly around her head, but in the end we couldn't control it and laughed until we cried, and after a while Gwen joined in too. Sister McIvor was soon out of her office to see what all the merriment was about. Gwen whipped off the towel, shaking her wet hair to show its new colour, which with time had turned an even brighter green. Sister McIvor took one horrified look and went back to the office shaking her head in despair, but we noted her shoulders were shaking with her own laughter.

The following morning, we were all dressed in our finery waiting for Dr Paul's round to begin. Everyone was displaying their recently washed and curled hair, all except Gwen, who wore a turban, strategically covering the whole of her head. When reaching her bed, Dr Paul remarked on her new style and asked why she was covering up her hair.

"It's a new look," she cheekily answered.

"French, I believe," Sister McIvor said in her usual sly way.

A Special Mark (Eva's Story)

When Eva was first brought on to the veranda she was quietly weeping with her head in her hands, taking deep sobbing breaths as if her heart was breaking. We were sympathetic; being admitted to the Sanatorium had been an ordeal for all of us – hard to leave the security of your home, family and friends, not knowing what to expect, or how long your enforced stay would be. But, with time we had responded to the little acts of kindness from our fellow patients, an offer to refill a hot water bottle, a loan of a magazine, or just a kind word; these gestures all helped to make a newcomer feel welcome.

Nothing at all could comfort Eva. She continued to weep for the remainder of the day and throughout the night, her head buried in the pillows which were saturated with her tears. She responded finally to Nan's softly spoken words of comfort, and allowed herself to be held, and soothed gently like a baby.

Eva became calmer, and lifted up her head to view the ward and the many concerned eyes that were looking at her with compassion. Her tear stained face was red and blotchy, making the large birthmark on her cheek even more prominent. Later when she felt composed enough to talk, she told us her sad tale. It touched our hearts, and by the time she had finished the veranda was awash with all our tears.

Thirty years earlier Eva's mother had been distraught when her baby was with a large purple birth mark across its right cheek, and not knowing any better she blamed herself, having had a fancy for beetroot during her pregnancy. Her mother-in-law, who had religious leanings, said it was God's way of marking the baby as a special child. Within a short time Eva's mother had come to disregard her daughter's blemish, and Eva was a much loved little girl who was sweet natured and well behaved. From an early age she had grown used to strangers staring at her, and then quickly looking away in embarrassment. Children pointed at her quite openly and asked her why she had such a funny thing on her face.

Growing up, she became more aware of the limitations that the disfigurement placed on her life. She felt self-conscious when meeting new people. She saw girls of her own age experimenting with makeup, watched them flirting with boys, and for the first time felt bitter about her own flawed looks. As she matured, her resentment changed to resignation, accepting that she might never have a boyfriend, marry, or have children. Men were always ill at ease in her company, trying over hard not to stare at her face, usually turning away, leaving an awkward silence behind them.

Robert was different. He had recently come to work in the packing room of the factory where Eva had been a machinist since leaving school. He was tall, solid and dependable looking, with a shy smile that lit up his whole face. He didn't glance away when meeting Eva for the first time, but looked straight into her lovely brown eyes and saw the sweetness of her nature and the warmth in her heart. They made a strange pair, he so tall and erect and she small and plump, but no one ever doubted their love when seeing them together.

Each had found their soul mate, and was completely happy, his big hand holding hers and a look of love on their faces. They had a short courtship, marrying as soon as they could. Her family were overjoyed to see her coming out of church as radiant and beautiful as any bride should be. The blissfully happy couple had rented a tiny cottage, one of ten huddled in the corner of a dark and gloomy yard. The dismal surroundings didn't dull their happiness. Together they cleaned, scoured, and decorated every room, making their first home special to them both. Their lives were uneventful but very happy. When Eva discovered she was pregnant they were both delighted, and made endless plans for the new baby. She had an easy pregnancy, but in the latter months developed a troublesome cough which at night disturbed her sleep, making her feel hot and fretful. Her doctor decided she should be x-rayed for the baby's safety.

The young couple's lives were shattered when the x-ray showed a shadow on Eva's lungs – she had Tuberculosis, and it couldn't be treated until after the baby's birth. The last two months of her pregnancy were filled with dread. She gave birth after a long and painful labour, and was allowed one brief look at her daughter, long enough to see that she was beautiful, and most important to Eva, completely unblemished. The baby was then quickly hustled away, and Eva transferred to the Sanatorium.

At this point of telling her tale she broke down again and wept. "They took my baby away," she sobbed. "I never held her, kissed her, or even touched her tiny fingers." Her suffering moved us all. She was tormented with her grief, feeling all the wretchedness of any new mother who has lost a precious child. Her milk came, painful, and leaking through the front of her night dress. She was given tablets to suppress it, but nothing could take away the aching need to hold her child and feed it herself.

Robert came every visiting day, always the first one through the door, his long legs striding across the terrace, not wanting to lose a second of the time they had. He would sit as close as he could get, his arms wrapped tightly round her, whispering his love, and telling her of their daughter's progress. They had called her Ann, and Eva's mother was taking good care of her. He always brought new photographs to show Eva how fast she was growing, both proudly passing them round the ward for everyone to look at. You could see how hard it was for him to leave when the bell rang and it was time to go. They clung together, only parting when Sister McIvor's discreet cough reminded them that visiting time was over.

Eva's kind nature and quiet humorous manner made her popular with everyone on the ward. She was a good listener, and you could always depend on her sensitive and caring encouragement when you felt dispirited. She rarely talked of her own sadness, hiding her heartache behind her ready smile, but in the silence of the night, muffled sobs were often heard from her corner of the ward, and someone would slip out of bed and hold her hand until she cried herself to sleep.

After eight months of bed rest she was allowed home for a long weekend, ostensibly to view a new council house that was being offered, but for Eva it was a chance to see her daughter, to hold her for the first time, and to show all the suppressed love she had for her. The baby, who by this time had a natural bond with its grandmother, cried at first when Eva picked her up, but instinctively seemed to recognise her mother's voice and nuzzled contentedly against her chest.

Eva came back to the ward transformed, her face shining with happiness. She knew it was going to be alright, her baby accepted her, the new house on the edge of the countryside was perfect, and she talked excitedly about the walks she and Ann would take in the lovely fresh air when she was well enough to go home.

Six months later she was allowed home for good. Robert came to fetch her and it was wonderful to see his tender loving care as he helped her into the taxi. We all cried with emotion as we waved her off, so pleased for her and the happy future that lay ahead for their little family.

Sadly, Eva died three years later of breast cancer, leaving Robert to bring up his daughter alone.

It seemed as if the fate of the little girl marked special had been long decided.

A Little Bit of Pampering

As Easter approached, Sister McIvor decided that as well as the veranda having a spring clean the patients needed sprucing up too. She told us that she had managed to persuade a beautician to come to the Sanatorium the following Thursday evening. As we later discovered she was not so much a beautician, but more of a shop assistant, who worked on the cosmetic counter of Timothy White's, the High Street chemist. She came to Sister McIvor's notice through a conversation with Sister Baker who ran the children's ward, who had a niece who had a boyfriend who had a mother that seemingly knew a lot about cosmetics. This being the shop assistant who had been badgered to give up her evening to educate us on beauty.

The poor woman when faced with Sister McIvor, who on her very next day off confronted her at the cosmetic counter, really had no ready excuse to refuse the request. An early supper was served the night of her expected arrival, and by 7 o'clock we were all tucked up in bed waiting for her with great anticipation. Sister McIvor had cleared the flowers off the central table, and laid a clean white tablecloth across it to make a makeshift counter for the beauty products she was expecting the woman to bring. She had also placed some clean towels on the arms of a visitor's chair, which was to serve as a seat to hold the patient who had been selected to be a guinea pig for the beautician's ministrations. We had all volunteered for this, and numerous arguments had flared up as to who would have the free session. Sister McIvor put an end to it by placing all our names into a sick bowl and getting Staff Nurse Levy to draw one out, saying she would never have arranged it if she had known we were going to squabble like children over it.

Eva won the draw, and we could see that she was deeply embarrassed by it all. She had never worn makeup, long ago discarding the special powder that she had been given as a young girl to hide her prominent blemish. Sister McIvor, seeing her distress, took another name out of the bowl. No such discomfort this time when Angie's name came up. She was delighted, welcoming the chance of a free make up, and possibly a manicure too.

When a small timid looking figure put her head around the veranda door we had no thought or recognition of her as the promised beautician. The rather frumpy middle aged woman looked quite terrified, and I think if Sister McIvor had not been right behind her, would have fled the Sanatorium altogether. But she was gently propelled on to the veranda, and had no choice but to smile weakly at the twelve pair of eyes that were gazing with dismay at her pleasant but unembellished face.

Sister McIvor didn't wear makeup, not even a dusting of powder to hide her freckles, and obviously had not thought it strange to produce a beautician who didn't either. We all began to get the feeling that our eagerly anticipated evening was going to be a big disappointment. We had also noted that the expected case of freebies had not accompanied her, and when she nervously opened her handbag to take out a small makeup bag, which looked quite ridiculous laid on the large ward table, we were positive that the promised make over was not going to materialize.

Angie, the chosen victim, was no longer feeling so thrilled about it; in fact, she was wearing more makeup than the so-called beautician had probably ever worn. But Sister McIvor, despite her own doubts, bravely introduced the frightened looking woman as Mavis Atkins, and giving us all a stern warning look, said that the beautician had kindly given up her free time to come and teach us how to apply makeup. I think she too had realised it wasn't going to be one of her better ideas.

Mavis invited Angie to sit in the chair, ignored the towels, and shakily opened up her makeup bag, having trouble with the fasteners as her fingers were trembling so. She took out some 'Ponds face cream' and cotton wool, and asked Angie to clean her stale makeup off. Her voice was quavering so much we couldn't hear a word she said. A tiny pot of blue eye paint was next to come out of the bag, in which she dipped Angie's finger and told her to smear it on to each eyelid. Next to appear was a small case of eye mascara, a pretty little case with a mirror and its own brush. She advised Angie to spit on the mascara, and then take up the brush and load it with the sticky black substance before stroking it on to her lashes. Angie's face was a picture; she had been doing this procedure for years, and we were all struggling not to laugh. I'm sure if Sister McIvor had not been glaring at us we would have exploded with the pent up mirth we were holding back. It could have quite easily been another disaster, like the Abbottsfield Colliery Male Voice Choir travesty the previous year.

We had all now come to the conclusion that poor Mavis was another one of Sister McIvor's victims who was utterly terrified of catching our bugs, having had no beautician's training, and whose only connection with makeup had been the selling of it, alongside aspirins and cough mixture. The poor woman had been coerced into this nightmare by a forceful, but ill-informed Sister McIvor.

Angie, also coming to this conclusion, helped herself to the lipstick and compact of powder, and quickly finished the job. Mavis, vastly relieved, told her to keep the makeup as a gift, and not even stopping to hear Sister McIvor's vote of thanks scurried off the veranda, I'm sure to go home to have a Dettol bath and mouth gargle.

Within minutes Sister McIvor had gone off duty, not waiting to hear our opinion on this latest scheme of hers. But at least we were able to let go of our suppressed laughter as Angie continued to plaster powder and rouge on to her face, ending up like a circus clown. She hadn't thought it a wasted evening, being very happy with the free makeup she had been given.

Gwen was intrigued by the Max Factor compact that had been used. It was called 'Creme Puff', and claimed to be a compressed foundation combined with powder. To the veranda's regular users of makeup this was something new, an obviously recent addition to the Max Factor range. Gwen was determined to have one and immediately wrote a note to her sisters asking them to bring one the next visiting day.

She couldn't wait to possess this marvellous new device, and counted the days until she would have it. The following Sunday her sisters were first through the door carrying a small brown paper bag. Gwen smiled happily to us all. Her sisters had managed to get her one. They crowded around her bed as usual, and we could hear the sound of tearing paper as Gwen tore the bag open, and then silence, followed by a scream of anguish.

The sisters stood back in alarm as Gwen held aloft the *cake* they had given her – a fresh creme puff.

A Gentle Giant (Miss Hopper's Story)

The appointment of a new ward orderly when Mrs West retired was of no great interest to us. She had been a sullen gloomy woman, quite indistinguishable from any of the other previous orderlies that Ward B had known. She was adequate at the job – the floor was daily mopped, and polished once a week, the morning drinks always served on time, but she had shown no interest in the lives or even deaths of the patients she served. Her main interest had been the movements of the hands on the ward clock – when they reached 12 p.m. she would don her coat, cram an old green beret over her frizzy perm and, clutching her string bag, would leave the ward without a backward glance. Arriving home, she would always gargle for five minutes with TCP. "You can't be too careful, working where I work," she would tell her friends.

That first Monday morning when Miss Hopper, our new orderly, arrived on the veranda, we all stared in astonishment. She was a positive Amazon, at least six foot two in her stocking feet, a raw-boned clumsy figure, wide shouldered, flat-chested, and with a head of unruly white hair which showered pins with her every movement. She stood at the ward door clutching a mop and bucket, shyly smiling at our gaping faces, her own curiously childlike, as if despite her fifty-four years, life had never really touched her.

Annabelle Hopper had viewed the Sanatorium rooftops all her life, having been born in one of the terraced cottages at the bottom of the hill, but had never before ventured through the large iron gates that separated the hospital from the outside world. She was the second daughter of Tom and Agnes Hopper. Her arrival had been somewhat a surprise, unplanned, and if truth be known, unwanted. One child was all they had intended, and Agnes always blamed the annual rose festival for the unsuspected conception. Tom was an enthusiastic rose grower, and that year his own special bloom called 'Sweet Susan' had won first prize. The bottle of wine that accompanied the silver rose bowl had proved more potent than expected, and as a result, nine months later Annabelle entered their lives.

She was a small, puny baby, with pinched features and a piercing cry. Whilst friends and neighbours patted her elder sister's pretty, curly head, and remarked on her perfect looks, they found themselves quite lost for words when peering into the pram at the new arrival, where Annabelle, her little face scarlet with anger, was screeching out her rage. "A good pair of lungs" was the usual comment before they hurried on their way. As she grew out of infancy Annabelle started to flourish, her parents becoming somewhat apprehensive about her rapid rate of growth. By her second birthday she had already overtaken her sister, and was going upwards at an alarming rate.

Agnes had always dressed the two girls alike, and whilst little Susan looked charming in frilly smocked dresses, her younger daughter was totally ridiculous. Her mother despaired of finding suitable clothes to fit her, especially now that she was reaching such Goliath proportions.

Annabelle herself was a happy, even-tempered girl, oblivious to her exceptional height and somewhat clumsy bearing. She went through her school years with a placid indifference to the mocking cruelty of the other children. When she left school, her father found her a job at the market garden where he worked. She loved it and worked as hard as any man, never complaining about the cold, or shirking from carrying the heavy sacks of fertilizer. She was still teased, but in a more friendly, matey way. In the evenings she was content to go home with her father, and after tea help him in the greenhouse. She became as passionate about rose growing as he, and they would spend long winter evenings studying seed catalogues and planning the following years' flower beds.

Once she was persuaded by her mother and sister to attend a Saturday dance held in the church hall. Her sister was soon besieged by partners, but Annabelle remained seated alone for most of the evening – she blissfully tapped her feet to the music, seemingly unaware of her wallflower status. A young church curate approached her and asked if she would like to attempt the Gay Gordons with him. He was soon mortified to find himself swung around the floor by what seemed a giant tornado. His energetic partner then pulled him in the wrong direction, causing an embarrassing multiple pile-up on the floor – the Gay Gordons being thereafter forever banned from the church hall.

Life went on as usual for the Hopper family, and other than Tom and Annabelle's prize blooms continually winning the silver rose bowl, nothing seemed to change. But then one cold winter's night Susan came home with her fiancé and announced that they were planning to marry and emigrate to Australia. Things then changed rapidly. After the wedding and the happy couple had departed, Agnes sank into a depression and took to her bed. It was decided, with little consultation with Annabelle, that she should leave the market garden and stay at home to take care of her mother and the house.

The routine of being nurse and housekeeper was tedious and frustrating for Annabelle. She missed the market garden and the banter of her workmates. Her only outlet now was working in the garden with her father. Each evening they would spend happy hours together, tending their rose bushes and preparing for the next rose festival. It was one such evening whilst kneeling side by side weeding, that Tom suddenly gasped, and keeled over into his precious rose bushes. A heart attack, the coroner said.

The next twenty years passed in blurred obscurity for Annabelle. She continued to care for her mother, who sustained her role of semi invalid, but now integrated it with her status of perpetual mourning. She had no perception of her daughter's grief and misery, and with the curtains in the cottage permanently drawn, the two women lived in a twilight world of incompatibility. The rose garden was neglected – Annabelle had no heart or inclination to tend it.

As her mother deteriorated into premature old age, so did Annabelle advance into maturity. She had lost her spontaneous gaiety and contented disposition. She shunned conversation and had totally retreated into herself. When her mother had a slight stroke, she felt almost indifferent. She nursed her, but with no feelings of affection, and when a second stroke caused her mother's death, she showed no grief at all. After the funeral was over, and she had returned to the solitude of the cottage, she experienced a sudden elation, running from room to room, pulling open the curtains and pushing the windows wide, letting the fresh air pour into the rooms.

The next day she walked up the hill, went through the iron gates and applied to work at the Sanatorium. Matron was not impressed by her interview, but not having had any other applicants and Mrs West due to leave that very day, decided to give her a chance.

Miss Hopper quickly became known to us all as 'Hoppy'. She never mastered her mop and bucket, and was forever dropping cups and saucers, and was frequently saturated by the bed pan washer, which as she said, "always turns awkward when it sees me." You always stiffened in frightened anticipation when she approached your bed, waiting for the inevitable jolt as she bumped into it, sending shock waves down your body and, whilst profusely apologising, she would career into the next bed with the same effect. Each morning we would see her peddling furiously up the drive on her father's old bike, her large body scrunched up, defying the gravity of the climb. She would come hurtling through the ward door, her too short orderly's uniform high above her knees, and a huge lopsided grin on her face, and a look of complete happiness.

She loved her job, enjoying every second of her time on the ward, resenting days off, spending them counting the hours until she could return to duty. She was interested in all our lives, sharing all our hopes and fears, and if anyone was feeling down, she would come into work bearing arms full of beautiful roses, their perfume filling the ward – feeling happy, she had gone back to gardening. She was passionate about her 'girls' as she called us, and we used her shamelessly. She ran our errands, spending whole afternoons in town matching someone's exact shade of embroidery silk. She would take our lists to the library, staggering back with bags full of books.

We constantly teased her, making fun of her clumsy attempts to do her job. She would trundle across the veranda with a bucket of coke for the ever-hungry fire, scattering bits of it in her haste. The polished floor had started to look dull, our drinks were always late and usually cold, and Sister McIvor was not happy at all about the fluff that her eagle eyes had spotted under a bed.

We could understand why Matron had to dismiss her, but felt so sorry when she left, her face stricken with misery, silent tears running down her cheeks, and when she turned at the ward door as if to beg a second chance, we all glanced away.

She continued to cycle up the hill each day, and whilst Sister McIvor was having coffee in her office, 'Hoppy' would sneak onto the veranda, anxious to check we were all well, and offering to do any shopping that was required. Sister turned a blind eye for a while, but when the illicit visits became excessive a strong line had to be taken, and Miss Hopper was ordered off the ward and banned from returning. A few days later she was spotted unsuccessfully trying to hide her bulk behind a pine tree opposite our veranda. Matron then prohibited her from entering the Sanatorium grounds, and the porter was given orders to turn her away.

After this, we all began to receive daily letters from her, long rambling missives that were often quite bizarre and sadly, we, in our own self-absorbed states of mind, didn't realise her need or recognise her desperation. A few weeks later we woke to find our beds strewn with rose petals and presumed she must have made her way unobserved into the grounds, and by the light of the moon climbed on to our balcony to leave a message in the only way she knew.

Two days later Miss Hopper was found by a concerned neighbour, hanging from a beam in her father's potting shed.

A Shared Romance

We had all noticed that Nan's brother was becoming a regular visitor. He never missed a single Sunday, and we all thought how lucky she was to have such an attentive brother. We had not failed to note how handsome he was too, and a few of us sat up a little straighter in our beds when he came through the door.

A few years younger than Nan, he was unmarried, and a trainee cooper at the brewery in town. Six months after Nan was admitted to the Sanatorium, he went off to do his two years National Service, which had been deferred until he had finished his apprenticeship.

There was a noticeable lack of anticipation on visiting day after he had gone. But Nan kept us informed of his progress, and suggested that some of us might like to write to him and his soldier friends, who were now on a special training course on the Salisbury Plains before being sent abroad.

Gwen and Ruth immediately agreed, and surprisingly Amy said she would too. They wrote that very day, and with a great deal of participation from the rest of us managed quite good, interesting letters. Of course, the main object of their penmanship was to have correspondence with Derek, Nan's good looking brother.

Within the week the three of them had received letters in return: Gwen's from a Welsh lad called David, and Ruth's a miss-spelt, torn page from an exercise book that demanded to know her bust measurements. Amy got the prize; she had a long letter from Derek, asking her to correspond with him. Nan said she thought Amy had been the object of his interest all the time, and he had pretended he was looking for pen friends for his pals in the hope that she would write.

For the next six weeks the correspondence was consistent, although Ruth's ardent soldier soon dropped communication after she had refused to send her measurements, which I might add was not out of embarrassment, but a desire not to inform him that she was not very well endowed in that area. We all told her that she should have fibbed, and when asked for a photograph, could have sent one of Gwen's ample figure.

Gwen's soldier was getting quite ardent in his letters, and we all looked forward to them coming as she always read them out loud. And we took much pleasure in helping her shape her replies, which generally became more spicy as the pen friendship flourished. But he then made the fateful mistake of sending his photograph, a pleasant enough lad, but not the Cary Grant of Gwen's imagination, being small of stature, and suffering with a bad outbreak of acne. Gwen's ardour quickly cooled, and racking her brains for a sympathetic way of ending the correspondence, came up with an answer. But she refused to enlighten us, and we only found out a few weeks later when Nan received a letter from Derek, telling her how angry young David had been when Gwen had written him to say that her husband and five children didn't like her writing to soldiers! But then Gwen was not renowned for her sensitive, compassionate nature.

Amy was still writing to Derek. She never divulged the contents of his letters or her own replies, but we noticed the weekly missives were now coming daily. She always looked up expectantly when Sister McIvor came on duty with the post in her hands, and a blush would creep up on her pale face when she received yet another one with a Salisbury postmark. She would read them over and over again, always with a secret smile.

They had been writing to each other for about three months when she received a letter that made her gasp out loud. He had written to say that he was being sent abroad, to join the conflict in Korea. She was shocked, never having visualized him going to fight in a war. The only consolation was the two weeks home leave he had been given, and his assurances that he would visit her as often as he could.

The first weekend he was due to visit she was so excited that she ran a high temperature and had to be put on strict bed rest, Sister McIvor even going so far as to say that she might not be well enough to have visitors. We all did our best to calm her down. Angie curled her hair, and helped with her make-up, Gwen lent her a treasured pair of earrings, and I ironed my best blouse to lend her.

Prompt at 2 p.m. Janet, who was on lookout by leaning dangerously over the balcony rail, saw him coming up the drive with his mother. Amy, looking as if she would like to disappear, took deep breaths, whilst we all scrambled back into bed, knowing Sister McIvor wouldn't let them in until we 'were all settled', as she put it.

He was even more handsome in his khaki uniform, and it wasn't just Amy's heart that did a flip. With a quick wave to his sister, he only had eyes for Amy and made straight to her side. We were all trying hard not to stare but it was difficult; we had wondered if he would kiss her, but he simply took her hand in his, and bent down to whisper something in her ear. She blushed and shyly smiled at him, but didn't remove her hand.

Nan and her mother were nodding their approval, and we all had beaming smiles as we looked at the happy couple, so engrossed in each other that they didn't notice our affectionate interest. After the bell had gone and he'd reluctantly left, she shed a few tears, so we tactfully left her to her dwell on his obvious regard for her.

The day before his leave ended, he asked permission to come and say goodbye to Amy, and as an afterthought to his sister too. He was allowed to come for an hour in the afternoon, and Sister McIvor with unusual delicacy told Nurse Bumstead she could screen off Amy's bed whilst he was there.

When he left, after a quick word with his sister, Amy got out of bed despite her strict bed rest, and leaned over the balcony to blow kisses to him as he slowly walked down the drive, and before he went out of sight she called out "I love you." We all had damp eyes, happy for her, but worried by her fragile figure as she coughed and wearily climbed back into bed.

He had asked her if she would get engaged to him as soon as he returned from Korea and she had said yes. We kissed her, and shared her happiness, feeling that we had all been part of this lovely romance.

Sadly, Amy died a few weeks before Derek came safely back after the war in Korea ended. But I like to think that he'd made her last year of life the best she'd ever known.

Sister McIvor's Holiday

Staffing was fairly constant at the Sanatorium, with only occasional change. Staff Nurses would come and go, and student nurses from the General Hospital did three month stints to help improve their knowledge of Tuberculosis. But Ward B had a permanent staff who, under Sister McIvor's guidance, worked well together and made an efficient team.

Without Sister McIvor's presence, the veranda would have run riot, or at least she seemed to think so, and was always very reluctant to have her days off or take an annual holiday. As she often remarked, things always seemed to go wrong when her back was turned.

The first week in August was usually the week she chose to take her holiday, and for days beforehand she drove staff and patients alike quite mad as she made long lists of jobs to be done, and went from bed to bed, warning us of the dire consequences if we got over-excited or forgot the rules that she constantly reminded us of. Before handing over the drug cupboard keys to Staff Nurse Levy, she would write endless notes for the relief Sister who was due the following day, most of which I'm sure would have taken the whole week to digest. At last she reluctantly left, and not wanting to show our delight too obviously, we waved from the balcony and wished her a good holiday, but she still lingered at the door, looking anxiously back, as if she couldn't tear herself away, or had a last minute hope that somebody would take a turn for the worse, and she would have to cancel her holiday and stay.

Finally, she left, and the sight of her retreating figure heading down the drive gave us all a feeling of relief. Bed rest patients immediately hopped out of bed, and the more active amongst us left the veranda and wandered into the main hall of Ward B to visit other patients whom we rarely saw, although Gwen and Ruth had spent time there and were familiar with many of them. It was good to see new faces and to have a change of scenery. And totally disregarding Sister McIvor's rules and regulations, we made illicit cups of tea in the kitchen whilst Staff Nurse Levy had gone down to the nurses' home for lunch. Nurse Bumstead turned a blind eye to our wayward behaviour, but would give a warning if senior staff were seen to be approaching, and we would all scurry back to bed, hearts loudly beating, and very much aware that our bugs were agitated too.

Rebellion against the rules was understandable. Sister McIvor kept both staff and patients under a tight rein, and we knew that the following day another of her ilk would arrive on the ward to cover for her absence. Usually it was a senior nurse loaned from the General Hospital in town, and so we took the opportunity to enjoy our freedom before she arrived.

The following morning we all eyed the door, anxious to see what dragon would be loaned to us this time. No one was prepared for the shock of seeing a man come through the door, but not just any man, this one was black. A giant of a man, with the blackest of black skin we had ever seen, in fact most of us had no recollection of ever having seen a real black man before. There was a stunned silence as he stood and surveyed the veranda and its open mouthed occupants. He was dressed in a white coat with the two blue stripes of his seniority sewn on to the shoulder.

For what seemed like hours he stood at the door, but it was probably only seconds, and then he came further in, and flashed us such a beaming smile that the whiteness of his teeth against the darkness of his skin quite dazzled us. He introduced himself as Nurse Errol Williams, and said he would be in charge of Ward B for the next week. His velvety voice was like soft treacle melting from a spoon, and still not one of us had said a word, too stunned to find our own tongues. Not only had we never seen a black man close up, but we had never envisaged a male nurse. At last Angie found her voice, and having met black American soldiers in the war was less astounded than the rest of us, and said, "Hi. Welcome to the madhouse."

He gave a deep throaty laugh, and came from bed to bed to shake our hands.

From that moment on we called him Errol Flynn. It was difficult to call him Sister, and he seemed to have no official title. The staff called him Nurse Williams, but we preferred Errol Flynn. Gwen said it for us all, when she remarked that this was going to be a good week. He was an excellent nurse, and ran the ward as efficiently as Sister McIvor, but he had a natural warmth that endeared him to us, and he was good fun. The only time he was serious was when Matron did her morning round, but even then he would wink at us from behind her starched frilly cap. In a free moment, he would entertain us by singing calypsos from his native Trinidad, and grabbing a clean bedpan from the sterilizer he would turn it upside down and beat out a rhythm to accompany his words. Within days we were unconsciously mimicking his lilting accent, and our limited record collection had been abandoned for his more rhythmic music.

He told us he had come to England in 1939 with some of his patriotic friends to join the British Army, and help fight Hitler. He had developed pneumonia the first week of training, and had never gone into battle. His illness had escalated into Tuberculosis and he had spent two years in a Shrewsbury Sanatorium. When recovered, he had decided to stay in England and train to be a nurse. He had been the first male nurse to train at a London hospital, and certainly the first black one. He hated the British weather and vowed every year to go back home, but instead went on to do his tubercular training, and seemed to have resigned himself to the cold winters.

The week seemed to fly, and soon we only had one more day left before Sister McIvor was due to return from her holiday. We made up outlandish stories to comfort ourselves – maybe she had met someone on holiday, fallen madly in love, and would marry him and never return. Ruth, who was going through a religious phase, suggested she might have given up on the wicked world and become a nun. And Gwen, ever practical, said she might have got run over by a bus.

But none of these happenings would have prevented Errol Flynn from leaving us. As a relief nurse, he was already booked to take charge of an Orthopaedic ward in Derby the following week. He made his last day fun by making up songs about each of us, and with a collection of bedpans we formed a steel band to perform them. Even Staff Nurse Levy had been won over, and rattled a tray of syringes in tune to our musical attempts.

When it was time for him to leave, he shook our hands, and wished us well before going off duty for the last time. It was if a sudden dark cloud had covered the sun. We all felt miserable without his cheerful face and laughter, and felt jealous of the patients who would be having fun next week at our expense.

Sister McIvor was back prompt at 8 o'clock the following morning. She didn't look suntanned, and had not lost the strained look that she always wore. In fact, Gwen suggested that she had perhaps not even been away, but had spent the week in her little cottage down the drive, spying on us with binoculars from her side windows.

She did a thorough inspection of the ward. Every nook and cranny was examined for the slightest trace of dust. She sent the casual student nurse to polish all the bedpans, saying they looked dull and finger marked, and then looked sharply at us as we started to snicker, which we quickly stopped when we saw her penetrating glance. Her nose always attuned to mischief led her to question each of us individually as to our behaviour the previous week. In fact the Spanish Inquisition could have learnt a lot from her tactics, and Amy burst into tears before she had even reached her bed. When she had learnt enough to her satisfaction she called a staff meeting in her office behind closed doors. They looked very chastened when they came out half an hour later, and we all trembled, knowing it would be our turn next.

But she came on to the veranda all sweetness and light. "I understand you had a very musical week," she said. "Perhaps I should invite the Abbottsfield Colliery Male Voice Choir back for a return visit, seeing as you enjoy it so much."

With that snide remark, she shut herself in the office for the rest of the day to scrutinise the holiday relief worker's notes. When it was time for her to go off duty she inspected our temperature charts, looking carefully for any abnormalities over the past week, and she must have found some as we were all put on bed rest for the next twenty-four hours, and booked in to have x-rays as soon as possible, putting the fear of death into everyone.

But secretly I was glad she was back. Despite the fun we'd had with Errol Flynn, I felt safer that she was once again in charge.

A Bright Star Shining (Gwen's Story)

Gwen was the youngest of five sisters, all curvaceous beautiful girls, with happy dispositions and flashing smiles, and much sought after in the village where they lived. Gwen, being the youngest, was adored and spoilt by them all, but despite such devotion she remained a sweet-natured, cheerful child.

The family was shocked and devastated when Gwen, still only a schoolgirl, was diagnosed with Tuberculosis, but accepted that it was not totally surprising as the disease was widespread amongst family members – both parents had been afflicted, their father dying of it, and their mother still undergoing treatment. They had numerous relatives who had succumbed to the illness. But her affectionate, loving sisters mourned that Gwen too had fallen victim.

She spent two years on the children's ward before being moved on her sixteenth birthday to Ward B. Her carefree ways and natural exuberance soon made her a popular patient, both with staff and fellow patients. She could always be relied upon for practical jokes, and her cheerful smile could brighten the most miserable day. Gwen was so buoyant, so enthusiastic, and so in love with living, but when I first met her she was slowly dying. By this time, she had already spent four years in the Sanatorium, and the disease showed no sign of abating. Her contaminated lungs were being eaten away by the most horrific of infections. Yet Gwen was never concerned with her future; she lived always in the present.

She ignored all the rules, always talked throughout the rest period, and was oblivious to her total bed rest status, wandering where and as she felt like. Sister McIvor had a softness for her, and would often turn a blind eye to her misdeeds. Only Gwen could entice that extra half hour at lights out, or cajole the night staff to make us all a forbidden cup of tea. Such was her power she could even raise a smile on Matron's granite features. Her biggest conquest was Dr Paul, the consultant who, when doing his monthly round, would always linger at Gwen's bedside, captivated by her cheeky grin, and maybe feeling a professional frustration at his lack of a cure for this enchanting girl.

She desperately wanted a boyfriend and her sisters, anxious to help, would coax young men to join them on visiting days, but these liaisons were never successful – the young men not choosing to have a dying girlfriend. She started to write to lonely young soldiers serving abroad, but once photographs had been exchanged her ardour would cool: "too spotty faced," or "they look gormless," she would complain. She ogled the porters, the gardeners and the window cleaners, and once terrified a visiting vicar by flaunting her ample bosom at his astonished face.

"I want a man," she would honestly say. "I want to be held and told I'm beautiful, I want to go to dances and parties. I want to flirt and be passionately kissed."

"We all do, love," came Angie's voice from the end of the veranda.

Gwen's well-endowed bosom was always a topic of conversation. She was painfully thin, but nature had endowed her with magnificent breasts that were so large it was a miracle her slender frame could support them – she was proud of their magnitude and would thrust them forward as she walked. We marvelled that their weight didn't topple her over.

She really came into her own on visitors' day. Despite the rule of two visitors per bed, Gwen's would be surrounded. Her ravishing sisters would arrive en masse, sitting on the bed passing round chocolates and bottles of Tizer. They would be joined by other relatives and friends, and visiting hour would be enlivened by their noisy laughter and gaiety. The ward was always quieter and darker when they'd left, and the aroma of their perfume lingered for many hours afterwards.

Gwen was an excellent mimic, and would brighten many a dull day with her clever impersonations of staff or fellow patients, some occasionally a little cruel, but always very funny. She would have us all in fits of laughter when she paraded the ward in the guise of Dr Paul. She would adopt his stance and voice to perfection, halting at each bedside to give an outlandish medical diagnosis, and to offer ridiculous remedies. But her party piece was when she donned an illicitly borrowed cap and apron to masquerade as Sister McIvor, with a convincing Edinburgh accent and the brisk walk that was so characteristic of Sister. She would stand by her empty bed and address her own misdemeanours, much to everyone's delight.

On one such occasion she was so absorbed in her role that she was unaware that the recipient had entered the ward, and was silently observing the entertainment. The sudden silence warned the impersonator, who spun round with a look of horror on her face.

Sister McIvor smiled with that special smile we all dreaded, and sweetly commented that she had been unaware that Gwen's origins were Scottish, or that she was a member of the nursing profession. Poor Gwen, blushing with embarrassment, handed over the cap and apron, and dived back into bed. Sister McIvor scrutinized the rest of us, who by now had sober meek faces, and warned us about our foolishness in laughing so much at such nonsense – "our bugs would feel very unsettled," she cautioned.

Sometimes even Gwen would feel down, she too having dark moments when she would lock herself in the bathroom and silently weep, but afterwards she would burst through the door grinning, with some new mischief already planned. Despite proving at times too high spirited for the more subdued patient, she was loved, appreciated, and admired for her spirit and refusal to accept defeat. The only time I saw Gwen cry was when Sister McIvor arranged a visit from her mother. An ambulance collected the sick woman and she was brought onto the veranda in a wheelchair; screens were put around Gwen's bed, and they had an emotional reunion – both realising that this was their final meeting.

Gwen's ambition was to go home for the Easter weekend, but her poor health made it extremely unlikely. She would try every possible trick to change Dr Paul's opinion. She weighed down her dressing gown pocket with pebbles on our weekly weighing day, but Sister McIvor was wise to this ruse and insisted she removed her dressing gown before stepping on the scales. Gwen's next plan also failed when the two heavy oranges stuffed inside her ample bra slipped out and rolled across the floor. But despite her lack of weight gain, Dr Paul took pity and allowed her home for an afternoon visit. A taxi was ordered to take her there, and four hours later returned a radiant Gwen who had enjoyed a wonderful afternoon.

After so many years Gwen had watched many patients come and go, but she bore no malice when she saw others cured and leave the Sanatorium. She would stand at the ward door blowing kisses and calling out, "Good-luck. Please don't forget me." As if anyone ever could.

Gwen died a few days before her 21st birthday. She had said her goodbyes to her family before slipping into a coma. Sister McIvor sat by her side night and day, holding her hand, and softly talking to her until her shallow breathing stopped. Staff said it was the first time they had ever seen Sister so anguished.

Gwen was missed by everyone who had been privileged to know her. With her passing a special light was extinguished, one that could never be replaced. Whenever I see an extra bright star in the sky I think of Gwen. The world was a poorer place without her.

Coronation Day 1953

Much to Sister McIvor's dismay, there was great excitement on the balcony in the weeks preceding Queen Elizabeth's Coronation. She was always doubtful about any activity that involved her patients' contact with the outside world. On reflection, she was against any animation on our part that, in her words, would stir up our bugs.

On this occasion, she simply couldn't ignore the forthcoming celebrations. Some lucky patients who were well enough were being allowed home to participate in the street parties that had been planned. And we that were left behind were determined to have our own share of the festivities.

Visitors stimulated our enthusiasm with their talk of parties and dances, and of television sets being especially purchased to watch the actual Coronation live. This was something special, something that had never happened before in our lifetime, and much to our resentment we were going to miss it all. We did our best to feel involved. On Sister McIvor's day off we made paper chains in red, white and blue and persuaded Nurse Bumstead to hang them between the beds. Sister didn't approve of anything that spoilt the neat lines of her ward, and considered streamers to be most un-hygienic.

We also used our weekly handicraft class to fashion raffia hats which we trimmed with patriotic ribbon. Despite being bedridden, we were determined to have our own celebration on the 2nd of June. Matron in fact was surprisingly sympathetic to our plight, and offered to bring over her own wireless set so that we could listen to the commentary, and hear for ourselves the young Queen make her vows. It had also been arranged for the cook to provide us with a party tea. We felt somewhat appeased by these considerate plans and began to see Matron in a new light, previously having thought her a bit of a dragon.

We could hardly contain our excitement. The only shadow on our expected enjoyment was the sudden decline in Amy. She had not been well since Easter and over the weekend Sister McIvor had taken the precaution of moving her bed into the corner next to the office door. I had come to consider Amy my best friend. We had become very close despite her being four years my senior. We had similar literary taste and as well as books, shared a slightly wicked sense of humour. We had recently asked Sister if our beds could be placed next to each other, and had spent a lot of nights since whispering and giggling together. I felt bereft now that she was at the other end of the veranda with the screens pulled around her bed, and I constantly badgered the staff to ask how she was.

It was my 16th birthday, two days before the Coronation and I wept when Eva gave me the card that Amy had made for me before becoming so ill. By now she had been moved into the small ward next to Sister McIvor's office and I asked if I could sit awhile with her, and because it was my birthday she gave me permission, but warned me that Amy might not know I was there, or even recognise me. I crept into the room and sat quietly by her side.

Amy seemed to be asleep, her flushed cheeks more hollowed than previously, and her breathing laboured. I took her hand in mine and whispered of all the things we planned to do when we were both well and released from the Sanatorium. I talked of her coming engagement to Nan's brother, and how I wanted to be her bridesmaid when they married.

When Sister McIvor told me it was time to leave I gently withdrew my hand, and Amy suddenly opened her eyes and gazed at me with a strange unfathomable look before sleeping again.

On the eve of the Coronation we realised that she was seriously ill. Dr Paul came after dark and spent some time with her, and Sister McIvor stayed on long after she usually went off duty. We were all subdued, straining to hear the forced, strangled breathing that was coming from behind the screens in the small room, and mentally willing Amy to fight on.

It was in the early hours of the 2nd of June that she gave up her fight. Coronation Day dawned, and as the veranda filled with early light we saw the empty room and knew that it had not just been a bad dream. We had lost Amy.

We didn't cry but simply stared at each other, numb with grief and very much aware of this devastating illness that we all had, and the toll it inflicted. Later we listened to the Coronation commentary on Matron's wireless set, but nobody wore their hat or had much appetite for the party afterwards.

The Coronation of Queen Elizabeth the Second only brings back very sad memories for me.

An Unexpected Visitor

I was shocked one Sunday afternoon to see the veranda's door flung wide, and a wheelchair pushed onto the ward containing my great uncle Mathew. Both patients and visitors alike stared open mouthed at his grand entrance. The usual chattering stopped as his journey down the veranda continued, all wondering whom he could be visiting.

But I knew, and couldn't believe he was actually here to visit me. Great Uncle Mathew was known as a recluse, and I believe had not left his fireside for at least twenty years. He was from a wealthy branch of our family, having made a fortune from manufacturing lino. He lived in a huge mansion on the Malvern Hills, with only his housekeeper and a manservant for company.

I had always accompanied my grandmother on her yearly visit to him, which was painful for both sides, he not liking relatives, and she detesting him. But I loved the house and its extensive grounds where I was allowed to freely roam, whilst they made awkward conversation over the tea and biscuits that his so-called housekeeper provided. "So-called," my grandma said, because she thought there was more to the relationship than just housekeeping, and not understanding her implication, I innocently presumed she was perhaps also his nurse.

Another reason for my enjoying the visits was the large crinkly five pound note that he always put in my coat pocket when we departed. "He likes you," my grandma said, "because you are quiet and well behaved." She took my sister one year when I had the measles, but to my delight she didn't get a five pound note, and was told not to come again.

In the latter years after the sudden death of his so-called housekeeper, the mansion was turned into a luxury nursing home with Great Uncle Mathew retaining a wing for his own use, living comfortably, with good food provided in the dining room, and keeping his privacy with the help of his manservant.

And now, unbelievably, here he was in the Sanatorium, dressed in his ancient Harris tweeds with a deerstalker hat perched on top of his balding head. His manservant, dressed in funereal black, was pushing the wheelchair whilst balancing a brace of dead pheasants on one arm, and a dripping basket of freshly caught trout on the other. The other visitors were craning their necks over the balcony to peer at his pre-war vintage Rolls Royce which was parked on the drive.

A few feet behind this entourage was my grandmother looking flustered and in shock. She later told me that she had gone for her usual visit, and he had been dismayed that she was alone, and had got quite agitated when she explained where I was. The following Sunday he had turned up at her door, or rather the manservant had, saying that Great Uncle Mathew was outside in the car and was demanding that she take him to see me. And despite their arriving at the Sanatorium with only a few minutes of visiting time left, he, with the manservant's help, had made it onto the veranda just before Sister McIvor rang the warning bell, with which she informed visitors it was time to make their farewells.

With his wheelchair pushed up close to my bed he scrutinised my face, and pronounced me to be looking well, and demanded to know why my foolish mother allowed me to lie here in bed when there was obviously nothing ailing me. At this point the bell rang, which he took to mean afternoon tea was about to be served, and called out that he would just have a cup of tea, no milk and one sugar.

Being somewhat belligerent and totally unaware of giving offence, he started to berate the other visitors who were obediently departing, loudly admonished them for going so soon, and he remarked how rude they were to leave just as tea was being served. Both patients and their visitors had never seen anyone like him before, and whilst the visitors reluctantly left, my fellow patients settled back into their pillows to enjoy the floor show.

It was not long in starting. Sister McIvor, realising there were latent visitors daring to outstay their welcome, strode down the veranda full of indignation. Seeing her crisp white apron in front of him, Great Uncle Mathew glanced up and said, "There you are, wench. Where is my tea?" and then turned to me and complained about the service, saying it wasn't much of place for me to be staying in.

I didn't dare raise my eyes from an intense study of the sheet in front of me, and there was a definite gasp of anticipation from the rest of the ward, staff and patients alike. To make things worse he took the blooded pheasants and basket of trout and thrust them into Sister McIvor's hands, charging her to get the fish gutted and the birds hung as soon as possible.

I slowly raised my eyes to look at her face but got no further than the blood stains on her immaculate apron, and quickly burrowed down under the bed clothes, blocking my ears against the expected explosion. She stood quite still, and as I was told later, with a look of utter disgust on her face as she clutched the well-meant gifts she had just been handed. Great Uncle Mathew, not one to be ignored, said, "Move yourself, wench. Don't stand there like a fool. Take them to the kitchen and get the kettle on."

A united gasp swept the veranda as everyone waited the result of this final insult. After what seemed like hours but was in fact a matter of seconds, Sister McIvor, with great dignity, or as much as you could show with two dead birds and a basket of trout in your hands, turned and walked slowly, and with great decorum off the ward. A few minutes later an orderly appeared with a tray of tea and biscuits, and almost with a curtsey offered them to great uncle Mathew.

After tea and a little chat, the usual crinkly five pound note was put into my dressing gown pocket, and I was kissed soundly on both cheeks, and told to get myself home as this was no place for me to find myself in. He then ordered the manservant to take him back to the car, and seemingly, as I again found out later, had spoken to the Ward Maid on his way out and told her to get rid of that gormless wench in the kitchen.

There wasn't a vacant space on the balcony as the Rolls Royce made its stately way down the drive. Then all descended on me once it was out of sight, demanding to know who he was, and would he be coming again soon?

There was no further sighting of Sister McIvor until she did her final round before going off duty. Once again immaculate with a crisp new apron, she went from bed to bed checking our temperature charts as usual. When reaching my bed, she smiled sweetly and said what a charming old gentleman my visitor had been, perhaps a wee bit eccentric she allowed, but she trusted he wouldn't be coming again. As an after-thought, she said his gifts had been passed on to a worthwhile cause, as the cook would hardly want them in her kitchen.

And with another sweet smile and a brisk goodnight, she went off duty.

Waiting for the Postman (Ruth's Story)

Ruth had occupied her corner bed at the far end of the veranda for nearly two years. She was small and dumpy, and despite having only recently celebrated her eighteenth birthday, already had a look of middle age about her. She came from the industrial Black Country, her voice having the unmistakable sing-song accent of that area.

Her family were susceptible to illness, their living arrangements leaving them predisposed to infection: she lived with her eight siblings and mother in a small, damp, bug infested cottage which backed onto the canal, the stench of which fought a daily battle to invade their home along with the potent odours of the adjoining glue factory. Her father had recently died of Tuberculosis, and as a result, the family were invited for regular check-ups at their local clinic, but were too poor to afford the tram fare. At this time, their only income was the small amount of money that Ruth's mother earned with her morning cleaning job, and the meagre wage that the corner shop paid Ruth. She hated the job, but was grateful to its owner for allowing her to make a late start, which enabled her to look after the little ones whilst her mother was at work.

The corner shop was situated next door to the post office, and all the postmen used it for cigarettes and sweets when returning from their rounds. Most of them ignored the small plain girl who served them, but one kinder than most always passed the time of day with her. She found herself looking out for him, and soon imagined herself in love. She questioned other postmen to find out his name and where he lived, and she would loiter outside his house on her way home.

A follow up medical check on the family found both Ruth and two of her younger sisters to be tubercular, and in need of hospitalisation. The little girls were taken to a Sanatorium in Shropshire, but there was no room there for Ruth, and she eventually found herself in the corner bed on Ward B's veranda.

She told everyone on the ward about her postman boyfriend, and how much in love they were. Her days were spent writing long passionate letters to him, and she never seemed distressed by his lack of response. Her only other pastime was knitting. She continuously

113

made him sweaters, starting a new one as soon as the previous one was finished. We all thought he must be the warmest postman in the Black Country. She had no photograph to show us, but from her description we thought him a cross between Cary Grant and Errol Flynn.

Being so far from home she had no visitors, but happily chatted to any spare one that came her way, taking as much pleasure from them as we did. She would make the same elaborate preparations for visiting day as the rest of us, curling her hair, and always wearing a frilly blouse which was bought from Nan's mother's catalogue, and which was of a particularly violent shade of purple. She seemed convinced every visiting day that her postman would come, but was never dismayed by his non-arrival. "He will have gone fishing in the canal," she always said, he seemingly being very fond of fishing.

And then one day to everyone's surprise, she received a postcard from him, passing it around the veranda with unconcealed excitement. Admittedly it was from her postman, it even had a picture on the front of the grimy post office, but we wondered at her elation when we read the other side – no loving greeting, just a brief message stating that he would be visiting the following Sunday afternoon at 2 p.m., and signed "Harold Tomlinson Esq."

Sunday morning, the whole ward was agog with anticipation. At last we were going to see the elusive postman. Ruth by contrast was quite calm, simply taking it for granted that he was coming. At five minutes to two, Sister McIvor checked the veranda. She straightened a few bed covers, wiped some imaginary dust from the central table, all the while aware of our suppressed excitement, but deliberately slowing down the process of opening the doors to allow the waiting visitors in – very little happened in her domain that she didn't know about.

The visitors poured onto the veranda, laden with bags and bunches of flowers, but for once they were ignored, all eyes focused on Ruth's bed, waiting for the postman to appear. She sat, quite serene, knitting in hand, completely unperturbed, knowing he would come. He slipped in unnoticed, a small middle aged unassuming man, slightly balding, so ordinary that nobody noticed him come. He sat stiffly by Ruth's bed, and it was some time before we realised who he was.

Our visitors were immediately hushed as we strained to catch the conversation from their corner – but there wasn't any. He just sat, whilst Ruth positively glowed with happiness. After ten minutes or so of no communication, he rose and left the ward. By standing on our beds and precariously craning our necks, we could see him approach a motorbike and sidecar, from which he extracted a petite lady whom he led by the hand back into the ward. They stood hand in hand by the side of Ruth's bed, and in a surprisingly loud voice he introduced her as his wife. She shook hands with Ruth, handing her a box of black magic and some wilting daffodils, and then still holding hands, they left.

We could hardly wait for visiting time to end, all longing to know what had happened, but when Sister McIvor had rung the bell and cleared the ward we were no wiser, Ruth just sat there, a blissful look on her face, and all she said was, "I told you he would come."

She never mentioned him again. The compulsive letter writing and knitting stopped. She took up quilting instead, and developed quite a crush on the visiting handicraft teacher.

Ruth stayed on the veranda for another year, but then her health deteriorated rapidly and she was moved into the small ward next to Sister McIvor's office on Christmas Eve 1954. She died the following New Years' Day in Sister McIvor's arms. She was just 20 years old. Rest in peace, Ruth.

The Easter Bride (Eileen's Story)

Eileen became a patient on Ward B a few days before Easter. She arrived by taxi on one of those glorious spring mornings that made you long to be well and out enjoying the early sunshine. She walked on to the veranda looking composed and very sophisticated. To the uninitiated her rosy cheeks and luminous eyes would lead you to believe her blooming, and in the best of health, but we all recognised the familiar signs: the feverish stare and her skeletal frame with its accompanying cough. We knew that despite her smart clothes and careful make-up she was in the right place. She was one of us.

She seemed aloof and very reserved, and despite being bedded next to Gwen, proved well able to withstand her barrage of questions. Gwen, always eager for news of the outside world, would usually demand answers from any newcomer. Eileen seemed to be indifferent to our friendly approaches, and abrupt in her response. We had all noticed the diamond solitaire she wore on the third finger of her left hand, and Nurse Bumstead, whose gossip was always to be relied on, told us that the new patient was engaged to a sports teacher at the local high school, where she herself was head of maths.

We had to be satisfied with this meagre information as none was forthcoming from Eileen. She seemed distant and totally alien to our close-knit sisterhood, spending her days reading or writing long letters, quickly closing her eyes and pretending to be asleep if anyone came near her. The first few days she spent lying on top of her bed dressed in her expensive looking velvet dressing-gown, her hair and make-up immaculate, but with a totally blank expression on her face as she stared aimlessly at the limited view of the world seen from her corner of the veranda.

It was Eva, quietly nursing her own grief in the early hours of Easter Saturday, who first heard Eileen's hushed sobbing. She slipped out of bed and went to sit by the side of the distressed woman. Holding her hand, she gently whispered words of comfort – this well-meaning sympathy turned the hushed sobs into a loud wailing. "It should have been my wedding day today," Eileen blurted out between spasms of heartbroken weeping. With many gulping sobs and flowing tears she poured out her sad story. By now we were all awake, but lying silently in the darkness, intently listening to her distraught choking voice. As we realised the grief she had been hiding, we all felt bad about the judgmental opinions we'd held of her.

She told of how she had planned and saved for two whole years for her special day. Her wedding dress was hanging in the wardrobe, a reception arranged, and a new flat decorated and ready to move into. She had known Johnny since teachers' training college, and had loved him for years, and was overjoyed when he asked her to marry him. Her recent weight loss and tiredness she'd explained away by the extra work she had been doing in preparation for her coming marriage, and also the excitement that was bubbling up inside her. Counting the days to the end of term, she had hardly noticed the mobile x-ray unit, parked with the Head's permission in a corner of the school playground, and agreed almost absent-mindedly to accompany the other members of staff for a chest x-ray during break-time. She'd been surprised but not alarmed to receive a letter a few days later asking her to attend the chest clinic for further tests. She presumed it was extra precautions because she was a teacher.

She left the clinic ashen faced, and deeply shocked. She had TUBERCULOSIS! She was not even allowed to return to school to pack her belongings or say goodbye, and had been told she was to be admitted to the Sanatorium the following morning – just three days before her wedding day.

Her story deeply moved her silent listeners. We all felt empathy and shed our own tears, enfolding her at that moment into the warmth of our shared adversity. Once her story was told, she lost her reserve and soon became a highly regarded member of our close knit veranda family.

Her Johnny came to visit her on Easter Sunday. All eyes assessed him as he walked the length of the ward searching for Eileen's bed. "Not bad looking," was the later census of opinion, although Gwen thought him a bit scruffy, dressed as he was in old corduroy trousers, with a well-worn tweed jacket with patched leather cuffs, and his fair hair flopping untidily over his forehead.

We were all amazed at the difference in Eileen when she saw him approaching. Her face lit up with a beaming smile, and she threw up her arms to embrace him. Suddenly she looked quite beautiful and vivacious. He gave her a cursory hug, obviously feeling embarrassed by the intense scrutiny he was under, but she clutched his hands, and kissed him repeatedly. He looked most uncomfortable by her obvious show of affection and ownership.

When he departed with at least another forty minutes of visiting time left, his rapid departure was observed by eleven pair of accusing eyes. We were all aware of how Eileen had longed for this precious time with him. But she hid her disappointment well, saying he had work to prepare for the new school term, a poor excuse we all thought considering they should have been at that moment touring Wales on their honeymoon.

It became clear over the next few weeks that Johnny didn't like visiting the Sanatorium. He never stayed long, and avoided physical contact as much as possible, his face always showing relief as he strode out of the ward. His visits became less frequent as summer came; the occasional one was always spent with a large handkerchief pressed to his mouth – all but Eileen realised that he was afraid, absolutely terrified of catching Tuberculosis. She was still madly in love with him and wouldn't listen to any criticism of his neglect. Her aim was to get well and be able to re-arrange her wedding day.

His visits dwindled, but he continued to send her loving messages via her mother or other work colleagues, always with flimsy excuses for his own absence. Rumours reached the ward that he had been seen out with a young domestic science teacher. We hoped it wasn't true, but felt sad to see Eileen's expectant look each visiting day, and her crushed face when once more he didn't come.

As summer ended, even she admitted that the relationship had become one sided. She talked long into the night about her fears and often cried herself to sleep. Much against everyone's advice she wrote him long letters, pouring out her love and hopes for their shared future. She received no reply, but at half-term she did have a postcard from France where he was staying with a party of schoolchildren and, according to Nurse Bumstead, accompanied by the domestic science teacher.

Then as the dark nights of winter approached she received a letter from him. He asked her to release him from their engagement as he'd fallen in love with someone else. Eileen was devastated. Sister McIvor gave her a sedative, and we took it in turns to sit by her side and offer comfort.

After a while her tears gave way to anger. She ranted against his deceit and the wasted years, but her biggest anger was against the BUG which she claimed had ruined her life. Angie, in her usual delicate way, said it for us all when she called out, "No Eileen. You should thank the bug. It showed you just what a little shit he really was."

Eileen made a slow but good recovery from Tuberculosis, and eventually with our love and support, from Johnny too. After leaving the Sanatorium she gave up teaching and trained as a nurse, specialising in chest infections. In her thirties, she married a Swiss doctor, and now lives happily in Zurich with her two children and six grandchildren.

Food for Thought (My Story)

I never made a conscious decision not to eat. It crept on me slowly, a combination of many things: feeling unhappy after a recent change of schools, a fear of growing up – at fourteen years of age the inevitable signs of puberty alarmed me. I unconsciously chose the most basic way to arrest my growth. I stopped eating.

Nowadays medical science gives a name to my affliction. It's called 'Anorexia Nervosa'. In 1952 in our rural backwater it was called, 'Eat your dinner, and don't be stupid.'

Unfortunately, it is often misnamed as the 'Slimmer's Disease', which is a totally misleading definition of the illness. My perception of Anorexia had no association with dieting, starvation being just a tool used to portray a state of mind, and the feelings of having no control over one's body or emotions. In times past, it was possibly the 'Wasting Disease' favoured by frustrated heroines in Victorian novels, or the 'Hysteria' popular in young girls of that period. In reality, it is a very serious, life threatening illness.

I had always been known as the 'Glutton' of the family, a reputation deserved, having once eaten a dozen jam doughnuts between the bakers' and arriving home, and how I loved fish and chips, chocolate eclairs, and bacon sandwiches, and had always greedily devoured my sweet ration in one go.

The early stages of my illness involved complicated and elaborate planning to disguise the fact that I was not eating, hiding food in handkerchiefs on my lap, or moving it around the plate whilst talking non-stop to distract my family's attention from the fact that none of it was being eaten. I would offer to clear the dishes before anyone could notice my untouched meal, or say I was not feeling hungry, or talk of the huge lunch I'd had at school that day. These tactics served me well for a time, the Anorexia victim becoming adept at devious behaviour. Another symptom I displayed at this stage of the illness was a desire to cook and bake in vast proportions for the rest of the family. I loved to see them eat, but couldn't allow myself to have any. Such is the nature of this complex disorder.

My weight was down to six stone before anyone in our busy household noticed. In fact, it was the dressmaker making the bridesmaids' dresses for my elder sister's wedding who first remarked on my thinness. My sister still swears I ruined her wedding photographs, which showed my skeletal frame to full disadvantage in a low-cut, primrose yellow, taffeta creation.

I was well entrenched in Anorexia by the time my parents realised that I had a serious problem, with acute mental and physical deterioration. At this time I was allowing myself three cups of black coffee a day, plus an apple on alternate days. The family resorted to well-worn attempts of bribery, coaxing, and even threats, all desperate measures to encourage me to eat. But this illness, like any other addictive obsession, is not open to reasoning nor has any awareness of family distress.

Anorexia puts you into a very lonely world. In its later stages, you become too weak to communicate, reserving your last remnants of willpower to survive each day. Eventually when my weight dropped to five stone I became bedridden, my days spent cocooned in my room, drifting in and out of sleep, and when awake, dreamily staring at the ceiling, imagining strange faces and shapes in the cracks. I lay in this twilight world for what seemed an eternity, no longer aware of time itself, accepting the light of day and the darkness of night as one. Once, I spent hours following the frantic exertions of a trapped fly, which was attempting to flee through a closed window. Feeling a kinship with its frenzied attacks against the glass, and its desperate need to quit the room, I was sad to see its surrender when, falling backwards on the window ledge, it gave an occasional twitch of life before its final end.

Strangely enough, my life was saved by developing Tuberculosis. A young locum filling in for our family doctor diagnosed the possibility, and a subsequent x-ray confirmed it. A week later I was transferred from my sheltered self-inflicted isolation to the daunting environment of a busy Sanatorium. My early days on Ward B were frightening; to find myself sharing the veranda with eleven other females was very intimidating. I was a shy, immature fifteen year old who had never found it easy to socialize, and the debilitating years of Anorexia had further decimated my social skills.

The miracle of my recovery from the eating disorder was totally due to those caring women, my fellow patients, who offered their friendship and gave me their unconditional love. The Tuberculosis was cured by a year's total bed rest, and the discovery of a new drug called 'Streptomycin'.

Fifty years later I can't vouch for my sanity, but I am well, despite still keeping a strict discipline on my eating, and having feelings of anxiety when forced to make changes. Clearly once Anorexic, you always remain a little wary of control. But I have been fortunate enough to have travelled the world and hopefully have given something back to society.

I have been lucky enough to have three wonderful children and two adorable grandchildren. Well aware that some of my friends on the veranda were denied this fulfilment, I am forever grateful for my recovery and my life.

The Good Samaritans

We were always kept busy on the veranda. Sister McIvor was well aware that idle hands made for idle minds, and in her way of thinking that produced bored patients, and bored patients stayed sick.

Although a stickler for our rigid rest periods and compulsory bed rest, she also spent many hours trying to think up schemes to keep us mentally active. We were not always happy with what she devised, and had hoped that after our previous brush with the male voice choir she would keep to her promise of arranging no more little treats. In fact we were quite content with each other's company, and didn't feel the need of outside entertainment.

Working within a very limited budget she had to rely on volunteers to come forward with offers of activities, and considering the nature of our illness many brave people did come forward and offer their services.

Mr Fretwell was a retired teacher who specialised in handicrafts. He would visit the veranda two afternoons a week, driving up the hill on a rackety old motorbike, its sidecar piled high with assorted materials and tools for his handicraft sessions. He was well into his seventies, but would stride down the ward with all the vigour of a much younger man. He would wear an old beige mackintosh, and a pre-war leather flying helmet that completely engulfed his head, just leaving room for a pair of ancient goggles.

He was a strange figure, and even more so when he spoke. His ill-fitting false teeth would waggle up and down, and occasionally they would slip out of his mouth altogether. He could have become a figure of fun, but in fact we all loved him. He was a genuine, kind man who had no thought of the danger of catching our bugs, and who was so patient with our often mediocre handicraft efforts.

He taught us a variety of skills, and we began to look forward to his visits. One of the first things we each made was a lampshade, stitching bright coloured panels around a wire frame, and finishing it off with a tasselled fringe sewn on the bottom. On completion, they looked quite professional, and we found a ready market in our visitors. An aunt of mine furnished every bulb in her ten-bedroomed guest house, including the lounge and dining room. We also stitched leather purses and shopping bags, all of which were in great demand. Everything of course had to go down to the fumigation hut before it was allowed out of the hospital grounds, but purchasers didn't seem to mind the faint smell that emitted from them for quite a while afterwards.

It had been one of Sister McIvor's better ideas, and we all benefited from the experience. Sadly Mr Fretwell had to give up his motorbike and visits when he suffered a stroke over the Christmas break, and we really missed him.

He was followed by an elderly spinster lady, Miss Robinson, who came to teach us quilting and tapestry work. She obviously was a little afraid of our bugs and whilst making a valiant effort to show us her skills, seemed scared to approach our bedside, and always kept a good distance away with a large man's handkerchief never far from her mouth. It was presumably, with regards to her marital status, newly purchased. And to our amusement we noted she had brought her own china cup and saucer for the afternoon tea that Sister McIvor provided her with, quite needless because the kitchen had separate crockery for staff and visitors. But in the end, despite her distant tutorage we managed to make a quantity of quilted satin cushion covers, which once again helped furnish my aunt's guest house.

Miss Robinson eventually found the steep hill leading up to the Sanatorium too much for her, and declined to visit us anymore. We had a little break after that, and could go back to idle gossip, and me to my reading again. But Sister McIvor not being one to give up easily, soon found another diversion for us. She induced two nuns from a nearby convent to make a weekly visit. Sister Maria and Sister Teresa had a passion for knitting woollen soft toys, and soon we were all clicking away with our needles making pink rabbits, yellow fluffy chicks, and for some odd reason, green monkeys. They were all being made for a good cause as the convent had a yearly fete at which they would be sold, after fumigation of course. The money made was used to support a missionary clinic in Africa. So we all felt good that despite aching fingers we were helping sick people who were in worse circumstances than ourselves. Also, my aunt wouldn't have much use for a green monkey.

For a while we had a literary figure visit us, who was introduced by her pen name of Brenda West. She was writing a romantic novel, and would read us a completed chapter every week, her voice always hushed and faltering as she reached the romantic bits. Although kind of her to come, the book was awful and we struggled to be enthusiastic after she had finished the chapter and looked up expectantly for our reactions. I never did see her name in print. She must have been really desperate for an audience.

We had regular visits from vicars and priests, all wanting to add us to their flock. A priest would come once a fortnight to have a mass and confession for the Catholics on the ward. Sister McIvor would screen off the end of the veranda and push beds down if necessary. She always attended herself, and a surprise participant was Angie, who later laughed it off saying that although she was a long lapsed Catholic, she thought it wise to take confession considering her state of health. Another surprise was Gwen asking for her bed to be moved down. Afterwards she said she wasn't exactly a Catholic, but she thought the priest was dishy.

We had one clergyman whom Sister McIvor had to ban from future visits. He was a little too warm and friendly with her patients, asking a shocked Eileen if she wore knickers in bed, and if so what colour were they? He'd also embraced poor Eva, feeling her breasts as he did so. Fortunately, he never came to my bedside; I would have had no idea of how to deal with him.

Many people were very kind and gave their time in a truly good spirit, despite their fear of infection, and I'm sorry to say that we didn't always appreciate it.

The Facts of Life

The Sanatorium was not just my home for eighteen months, it was also an extension to my education, what you might call a finishing school. My schooling had ended abruptly when I became seriously ill with Anorexia, and although my new studies were not academic, they proved a wonderful introduction to adulthood, with all the mysteries of life explained.

It was a very naive fifteen year old who moved into the end bed on the veranda, but it would have been impossible to have remained so innocent whilst living with eleven women of such different backgrounds and maturity.

My indoctrination was not immediate. Many times my ignorance and gullibility caused amusement, and later some embarrassment to me. At first the evening chats after Night Sister switched the lights off went completely over my head. In fact the whispering voices usually lulled me to sleep; perhaps just as well, as it was usually the married women who initiated the sexual element. I remember much laughter and teasing when they received a weekend break at home, and the whispering would intensify on their return.

My most mortifying experience came when I finally discovered the reason for Sister McIvor's monthly bedside chat. She would go from bed to bed always asking the same question, jotting the answer down in a little red book. When it was my turn I simply answered with the same reply that everyone else made – "Yes. I'm normal, thank you," the query having been, "Have you had your monthly?" I had no idea what she was talking about, and was too embarrassed to ask, so thought it safer to give what seemed to be the accepted answer.

Anorexia had halted my normal development and it was to be another year before I had valid reason to be asked the question. When the day came that I finally menstruated, I rushed to Sister McIvor's office with all the fear and panic of my ignorance. I found her to be so kind and instructive that I felt myself lucky that she was the one to discreetly enlighten me. The following month I gave a resounding, "Yes, I am normal, thank you." And as she left my bedside she gave me a wink and a conspiratorial smile.

My body, released from its burden of Anorexia, soon showed a sudden spurt of development, and once again Sister McIvor stepped in and explained the natural evolution of the female body. In fact, I was probably better informed at this stage than most of the women on the ward.

Listening more carefully to the evening conversations, in particular Angie's contribution, helped fill in the gaps that Sister McIvor found prudent to omit. Angie would talk quite openly about her gentlemen friends, and their various quirks. I suppose in different circumstances she would have been thought shocking or even called a tart, but on the veranda she was just our Angie, and was loved without being judged.

Occasionally when receiving their hours up, some patients would go for a ride in the country with their boyfriends or husbands, if they were lucky enough to own a car. Afterwards, when coming back on to the veranda, they were discreetly questioned about their trip out, but no one remarked on their flushed faces and creased clothing.

These trips out were eventually stopped when one caused an unfortunate incident. Sally was already a patient on the ward when I was first admitted. She was a very attractive girl with lovely auburn hair. When she gained her four hours up, her boyfriend would come and collect her in his car to go out for an afternoon spin. Unfortunately, she was not able to give Sister McIvor the right answer when the next monthly question was asked.

A few days later she left the veranda. It was whispered that she had gone for a private abortion. She never came back to the Sanatorium, going on instead to a convalescent home down south. One of her patients getting pregnant was Sister McIvor's biggest fear; understandable when you think of poor Eva's predicament, having to hand over her new born baby as soon as it was born.

Previous to the cancellations of car trips, was the scandalous episode of the huts. These in fact were pretty little self-contained chalets dotted around the spacious grounds, and used to house patients who were almost ready to go home. In theory, they were a stepping off point between the wards and finally leaving the Sanatorium. They would allow the cured patient privacy, and a chance to adapt away from the restrictions of the ward.

This idea too was discontinued when a female patient in one of the chalets was discovered by Night Sister to have a male sharing her bed. From that day on women were no longer allowed the privilege of moving into one, although the male patients were still permitted to enjoy the freedom of them – definitely a case of gender favouritism, and causing much grumbling on the veranda.

Occasionally there would be mild flirtations between male and female patients. These usually consisted of nothing more than passing notes from one ward to another. This was helped by the x-ray machine being housed at the back of Ward A, the men's ward – we all had regular visits there and had to pass across their veranda to reach it. Many a brief assignation was started in this way, never going further than a quick chat or the exchange of jigsaw puzzles and books.

Gwen, flashing her dazzling smile and big bust, had numerous conquests over the years, but these never went past the cheeky notes she received, and the numerous unsigned Valentine cards that came her way.

One romance did blossom, the couple meeting whilst walking in the grounds after receiving their hours up. According to veranda legend, it had led to steamy encounters in the thick undergrowth, something that even Sister McIvor's fertile imagination had not anticipated. But happily it had ended well, with them eventually getting married, the bride coming up to the Sanatorium in her wedding dress to see her old friends who were still tied to their beds.

Despite illness, the unquenchable spirit of my fellow patients made my time on the veranda a valuable experience that could never have been gained at a normal finishing school.

Going Home

The one aim for everybody on Ward B was to go home. This was always our goal: to be able to leave the sometimes suffocating atmosphere of the veranda, and to be a normal human being again; to do simple things like getting up in the morning and dressing, go shopping, or meet friends and visit family, and most of all, to feel free of the cloying smell of illness that so often pervaded the ward.

Despite being happy for the lucky ones who were able to leave, there was always that feeling of envy that it wasn't you. After someone left there was always a time of silence when we all lay back in our beds, reflecting on our own hoped for release. And always that fear that it might never happen.

Before your final discharge there was a procedure of half days out, which was later followed by a full weekend spent at home. I was never sure if that weekend was to test the patients' strength, or perhaps to verify the relatives' welcome. The long residence on the veranda had not only brought changes to us, but our families too had learnt to live without our presence and had become used to our absence, accepting the weekly visits to the Sanatorium as normality.

We all looked forward immensely to the weekenders' return, looking on them as intrepid explorers coming back from this other land that we no longer had a place in. We longed for information of the outside world, and harassed them with questions:

"Did you go to town?"

"Or the pictures?"

"And what did you eat?"

Some, more brazen, asked the married women for more intimate details, the latter usually discussed after lights out when the darkness could spare their blushes. In this way, we all shared in the excitement of their going home.

After what seemed a lifetime my own weekend came. When Dr Paul told me that I could go the following Friday and stay until Sunday, I was overjoyed. In retrospect, I think the biggest pleasure was the planning of it, and the huge expectation of what it would mean. Everyone helped with my wardrobe; a silk blouse was lent, and precious stockings handed over without a qualm. On the Thursday night before my trip I was given a face mask, and a manicure, whilst Gwen shampooed and curled my hair.

My father appeared prompt at ten o'clock the next morning to collect me, and with Sister McIvor's cautions and my fellow patients' best wishes ringing in my ears, I followed him out of the ward to the car. Looking back as we drove away, I could see faces at the window and hands to lips blowing kisses, and a sudden rush of tears came to my eyes. I knew exactly how they were all feeling, watching yet another friend leave.

Arriving home was a massive anti-climax. Everything was familiar and yet so very strange. My parents seemed to be handling me with care as if I might collapse and perish in front of them. My younger sisters were shy and held back as I entered the house, and my elder sister seemed almost put out by my return. I found out later that she had occupied my old bedroom whilst I had been away and had reluctantly given it up for the weekend.

After lunch, I wandered aimlessly around the house and garden, noticing all the changes that no one realised I had missed. I felt as a stranger would feel, uncomfortable in an alien place.

That first night I felt so alone, no comforting whispering between beds, and the darkness of my room seemed full of shadows, lacking the flickering light of the veranda's stove. I also felt overwhelmed by the four solid walls that seemed to be pressing in on me. I jumped out of bed and swung the window open as wide as it would go, and despite the cold night air felt able to breathe at last.

I woke the next morning to find utter silence, everyone in the house on their best behaviour, all creeping about trying not to disturb me. But I wanted to hear the remembered sounds of home, my sisters having their usual childish arguments, and my parents talking in their normal voices – not this dismal solemn performance, almost as if someone had died. I felt very alone and wanted to be back on the veranda with my other family.

My mother suggested a trip to town to buy me some much-needed shoes. It felt strange to be driven down streets that were so familiar, yet so far away from my recollection or the reality of my present world. I was afraid of the busy thoroughfares, and too timid to cross the road with its fast, noisy traffic speeding in front of me. I found it an effort to walk into shops or to meet old acquaintances who wanted to gossip, and marvel at my new healthy-looking appearance.

The weekend seemed to last for ever. I was happy to see my family, but I had no feeling of belonging to them. My heart was still on Ward B with all my dear friends. My father drove me back on Sunday afternoon, telling me not to fret because I would soon be home for good. But as we turned in through the gates my heart lifted, and when back on the veranda with all the women greeting me with so much warmth and love, I really did feel I had come home.

Cured

Two weeks after my weekend home Dr Paul did his usual round. He spent longer than usual at my bedside, intently studying charts and my latest x-ray. At last he glanced up and smiled at me. "Well, young lady," he said, "you are cured, and can go home for good."

I couldn't believe my ears. I was cured, my lungs were clear of Tuberculosis, and I was free to go. As soon as Dr Paul had left the veranda everyone clapped and cheered me. The staff came to offer their congratulations. Sister McIvor said she would ring my parents, and as soon as the paperwork was done I could go.

I still had some difficulty in grasping the fact that I was leaving the veranda for good. Part of me was exhilarated by the news, but I was also quite terrified. This ward had been my home for the last eighteen months, and fellow patients were my closest kin. I simply had no conception of a life without them, or the security of the Sanatorium.

Sister McIvor said she had spoken to my mother, and my father would be coming to collect me within the hour. I got dressed, and felt naked without my pyjamas and dressing gown on. I tried to pack but was trembling so much I couldn't still my hands to fold the clothes. I shared out the remainder of my belongings, giving Gwen the good luck charm that had hung over my bed rail since the first week of my admittance, and Angie said she would always remember me when cuddling the little fluffy dog that I gave her.

Sister McIvor called me into the office to sign the departure form. She smiled warmly at me, and said she hoped I would remain well and take good care of myself, and surprisingly gave me a hug. Staff Nurse Levy and Nurse Bumstead both kissed me and wished me well.

My father's car pulled up outside, and I knew it was not just a dream. I was actually leaving the veranda for good. He was beaming when he came on to the ward to carry my case. I asked him to give me a few minutes to say goodbye to my friends, and he went out to sit in the car, realising that it was an emotional parting for me to make.

I went from bed to bed, and hugged and kissed each of my fellow patients. Tears were streaming down my face and I had no words to say to them, or they to me. I stood at the veranda door looking down

132

the ward, my bed already stripped and being prepared for a new intake, and I felt jealous of that unknown person taking my place. I knew that these women I was leaving behind would always be in my heart, and I would never forget any of them.

Sister McIvor escorted me to the main door, and I had a sudden flashback to that time eighteen months ago when she greeted me in the very same spot. I had been so afraid, not wanting to enter, but now I was a different person, a year and a half older, well in health, and cured, not just by Streptomycin alone, but with the love and compassion that eleven wonderful women had given me.

As I climbed into the car they all stood on the edge of the balcony to wave. Through my tears I could see their smiling faces, and as my father drove down the hill I turned for one final wave, feeling such a sense of bereavement that I thought my heart would break.

It took a long time for me to adjust to leaving the Sanatorium. I felt like a square peg in the proverbial round hole. Whilst I had been getting cured my family had lived their lives. My elder sister had married and was expecting her first baby, my younger sisters had grown and I didn't have the same relationship with them as before. My parents were unsure how to deal with me, afraid I could sink back into illness if crossed. And I was just terribly lonely.

At first I still lived by Ward B rules, looking at the clock every few minutes, knowing exactly what everyone would be doing at that moment. Although I was physically back home, mentally I was still a patient on the veranda.

My parents wanted me to go back to school and resume my interrupted education. I did go back for a day at the beginning of the new term, but quickly realised it was not the answer to my loneliness, and I had long outgrown the childishness of my contemporaries.

For a while I made frequent visits back to the ward, climbing the steep hill with the other visitors, and feeling the familiar sense of security as I passed through the doors. These visits were never successful. I no longer felt part of the close-knit community, and had become just another visitor from the outside world.

Sister McIvor stopped to speak to me as I was leaving the veranda after one of these abortive visits. She invited me into the office, asked about my health and then very gently advised me not to repeat my visits. She said it was time for me to leave the Sanatorium behind, and to get on with my life. Wise words, and from that moment I let go of the veranda for good.

It was not easy adapting back into society, or even becoming part of my family again. But with time I became reconciled to being cured.

Memories

I recently went back to the Sanatorium, half a century since my last visit. Now empty and deserted, it awaits the future planned development of its valuable acres. It had been standing derelict for many years, outliving its usefulness with the decline of the disease, used for a while as an annex to the old infirmary, but finally sharing its redundancy when the big new medical centre was built on the edge of town.

I couldn't allow my memories to be bulldozed and put aside without one final goodbye, so after all those years I found myself climbing the steep hill up to the Sanatorium. I paused breathless at the iron gates that led into the hospital grounds, marvelling at the stamina and loyalty of all those bygone visitors who had toiled this same route winter and summer alike, laden down with heavy bags of clean washing, books, and tasty titbits with which they hoped to tempt our vanished appetites. Such faithful, not always appreciated, family and friends who never ever let us down!

I hesitated at the gate, memories already coming thick and fast, and feeling nervous of the ghosts I might arouse or the painful recollections I could expose, many of which I'd successfully buried.

The lodge gates were rusty and squeaked as I pushed them open. The lodge itself was empty, its windows boarded up, and graffiti sprayed across the walls. The once meticulous grounds were overgrown and neglected, but the damp earthy smell that pervaded the air was suddenly familiar – the shrubbery had always been dark and fetid smelling, the heavy tangled bushes clinging together in search of the light that the tall trees had robbed them of.

The long drive that curved its way through the grounds looked shabby with potholes and persistent weeds that had forced themselves through the thinning layer of gravel. I remembered it with its neatly trimmed borders, raked every day by the assistant gardener, and rigorously inspected by Matron as she swept along it to do her ward rounds. Without thinking, I turned and took a shortcut through the shrubbery which, despite being tangled with weeds, still showed a path that many feet had trod. It took me higher up the hill and as I came out of the dense trees back onto the drive, I caught my breath. There in front of me was Ward B.

It looked exactly as I knew it would, the way it had always looked, the long low building with its wide verandas, perched high on the hilltop, the massive pine trees still standing guard. I was too far away as yet to see what the ravages of time had done to it, but I could see what neglect and vandals had done to Sister McIvor's cottage. Set back a little from the drive in its own once pretty garden, it was now dilapidated and abandoned. She would have been incensed to have seen the broken windows, the gaping holes in her roof, and most of all the four letter words that adorned the peeling paintwork of the door. I marvelled that anyone would have had the audacity to dare to write anything so sordid on her property. My lips twitched at the thought of her irate indignant face if she could see it, but she had long since passed away, having spent her latter years ruling the roost and making the staff miserable in a south coast retirement home, where she had reluctantly died, leaving her substantial fortune to the benevolent fund of her lover's Scottish regiment.

I hesitated before approaching Ward B. A wind as cold as ever I remembered was sweeping across the hill and whistling through the empty rooms. Climbing the steps, I was swept back in time to the early fifties, and saw again the shy frail figure that I'd been, so scared, almost too weak to walk, unaware then that this place would be my home for the next eighteen months. Now I look back on that sad figure and know that Ward B was the making of her, the values it brought, and the love and strengths it gave, were precious gems that have sustained me throughout my life.

The wide door was slightly ajar, and stepping over heaps of rubble I crossed the now tarnished, but once immaculate tiled hall, and walked down the long corridor, passing through the double doors at its end which led onto the veranda. The winter sun was beaming across the open room, making the dust rise and float upwards in a sparkling haze. I had a sudden vision of Gwen, dancing and frolicking between our beds, a mischievous look on her face, her magnificent bosom leaping from her pyjama top with the eager tautness of her youth. Gwen now dead for half a century, but whose spirit is still strong in this dusty room.

If I close my eyes everyone is here – I can hear the chatter and the laughter, but also feel the sadness too that was always present. I can almost hear the rustling of Sister McIvor's starched apron, and the firm tread of her sensible black shoes as she trod the wooden floors of the veranda – always sharp of tongue but totally dedicated to our wellbeing.

I was amazed to see the old black leaded stove, still in its usual place at the head of the ward, battered and rusting, its door broken and hanging by one hinge – the remains of a fire in the long dead ash inside. How it used to roar on windy nights, its chimney shaking with the ferocity of the burning coke! And what comfort it gave in the dark of the night when its fiery embers lit the ward! Birds were now the veranda's only occupants, flying through the empty echoing room, screeching and twittering like ghostly reminders of its previous inhabitants, leaving their droppings on the once pristine floor, and nesting in the crumbling rafters of the damaged roof.

I closed my eyes one last time and saw the veranda as it used to be – the rows of beds each separated by the lockers that were our only privacy, the green winter bedspreads which were our shield against the winter elements. Standing there, oblivious to my ravaged surroundings, I felt all the old feelings of security and warmth that had been evoked by my memories. My thoughts were of all my fellow patients – their presence still inhabiting these rooms.

I had seen enough. I'd laid my ghosts to rest; it was now time to let them go. The bulldozers would soon do their work and new houses would appear on the empty site. Families unaware of its past would make their own memories here.

If on a blustery night they hear soft weeping, they will blame the tall trees blowing in the wind, and if they see shadows in the moonlight, they will think them a trick of the light. But I know that this place has too many memories to ever rest in peace.

Editors' Note

Tuberculosis has been a fact of human life for thousands of years affecting young and old, rich or poor. TB is an unusual disease in that young and fit victims would appear to fight it off but, unlike measles or chickenpox, TB could come back with a vengeance in later life, often after a debilitating attack of some other disease. We know now that TB never truly went away. If someone survived the infection, the 'bugs', confined behind protective tissue within the lungs, were contained. If unfortunate circumstance breached these protective tissues, the individual could relapse and suffer subsequent reinfection.

In many communities TB affected everybody but was held at bay by the fittest who could live full and accomplishing lives. Eventually, doctors realised the safest course of action was to separate out those clearly suffering from active disease.

For many years until the availability of Streptomycin, the only known 'cure' was fresh air and bed rest. In the twentieth century, isolation hospitals, or Sanatoriums as they were known, were built in the countryside, where sufferers could be treated without the danger of infecting others. Until then, whole families could contact TB.

In many countries TB is becoming a problem again as antibiotics become less effective or too expensive; or in countries without a universal health care scheme. As a consequence the disease is becoming resistant to antibiotics and is now endemic amongst the very poor, the undocumented and the uninsured. Rita's memoir still has relevance.

In *A Shadow in My Life*, Rita writes candidly about her struggle with anorexia.

If you are affected by any eating difficulties, and are concerned about yourself or another, please reach out.

In the UK, contact:

National Centre for Eating Disorders, 54 New Road, Esher, Surrey, KT10 9NU. Call the helpline, Monday to Friday from 9.00 am - 5.30 pm: 01372 469 493 or 0845 838 2040

Effective help and treatment for sufferers. Excellence in training for professionals.

You can also use the online contact page:
http://eating-disorders.org.uk/contact-us

In America, contact:

NEDA: Feeding hope.

National Eating Disorders Association. Call the confidential helpline, Monday to Thursday from 9:00 am - 9:00 pm and Friday from 9:00 am - 5:00 pm (EST): 1-800-931-2237

NEDA is a leading non-profit in the field of eating disorders, reaching millions of individuals and families every year. Visit them on www.nationaleatingdisorders.org.

Other novels, novellas and short story collections available from
Stairwell Books and Fighting Cock Press

Carol's Christmas	N.E. David
Feria	N.E. David
A Day at the Races	N.E. David
Running With Butterflies	John Walford
Foul Play	P J Quinn
Poison Pen	P J Quinn
Rosie and John's Magical Adventure	The Children of Ryedale District Primary Schools
Wine Dark, Sea Blue	A.L. Michael
Skydive	Andrew Brown
Close Disharmony	P J Quinn
When the Crow Cries	Maxine Ridge
The Geology of Desire	Clint Wastling
Homelands	Shaunna Harper
Border 7	Pauline Kirk
Tales from a Prairie Journal	Rita Jerram
Here in the Cull Valley	John Wheatcroft
How to be a Man	Alan Smith
A Multitude of Things	David Clegg
Know Thyself	Lance Clarke
Thinking of You Always	Lewis Hill
Rapeseed	Alwyn Marriage
Tyrants Rex	Clint Wastling

For further information please contact rose@stairwellbooks.com

www.stairwellbooks.co.uk
@stairwellbooks